KU-018-071

Contents

Foreword
by Deborah Moggach

When it comes to technology, I'm a Luddite. This stems from several things: cowardice, laziness, monetary meanness. It also stems from something deeper, something that every writer will recognise: a magical reliance on the familiar. Our bond with our tools is a profound and secret one; if we venture into the new technology, will we somehow lose our voice? Ten years ago I took a huge step and bought a computer. It terrified me. A helpful expert told me how to work the few buttons I needed – typing stuff into it, erasing and storing. I still haven't learnt how to shift passages of text and simply type them out all over again. My computer can do a million things and I'll never know what they are, for I've never opened the two vast manuals that accompanied it. But it's become familiar, my ally. A small step, I guess.

I still haven't got into the Internet but I'm gearing myself up to do so. Everybody goes on and on about it, and I'm starting to feel pathetic for not yet mastering it. Jane Dorner's book will be the catalyst. In her earlier *Writing on Disk* she managed the near-impossible: to write a friendly, demystifying guide to something which is there to help us, rather than daunt us. She made computers companionable. Her guide to the Internet is equally invaluable, for she understands something which is often forgotten in the blizzard of technology that threatens to engulf us – that we've got to have something to say in the first place, and no amount of chip-based wizardry will disguise that. With the author's needs and concerns in mind, she leads us into this new world – probably not new to you, but new to me. I look forward to joining you there soon.

The author

Jane Dorner has published 18 books, as sole or co-author, worked as a writer and editor for many years and has latterly turned to web publishing. She is on the Council of the Authors' Licensing & Collecting Society, the Board of the Copyright Licensing Agency and other writers' committees. Involvement with these organisations led to close concern with the techniques and problems of electronic publishing as they affect writers and journalists.

She became involved in the new tools for authors when writing a report for the British Library called *Authors and Information Technology* and while editing *The Electronic Author* for the Society of Authors (now subsumed into *The Author*). She also wrote a regular technology column for *Writers' News* as well as the successful *Writing on Disk*.

When Jane Dorner opened her first email account in 1993, she knew only four other people who were online. Her experience then greatly expanded as she went on to include reviewing word-related software products of all kinds, through which she acquired a well-grounded working understanding of their impact on writers in the Information Age. This has enabled a sure-footed approach to the slippery issues raised by the new technology and offers excellent pathways to 'the tools of the trade'.

She has a balanced view of what the Internet offers and is neither over-enthusiastic nor dismissive. While cautioning against inherent constraints, she is open to the new opportunities that arise out of the interaction between technologies and the creative mind.

Professional and personal details are on her own site at http://www.editor.net.

Acknowledgements

My thanks to everyone who has talked to me, and taught me, about the Internet – more than I could possibly name from all over the world. Many are quoted and acknowledged in the book. A special thanks to writer colleagues (or teachers on writing courses) who read and commented on the book in its earlier drafts: Susanna Gladwin, Nick Faith, Feona Hamilton, Roy Johnson, Antoni Marianski, Vivienne Menkes, Charles Palliser and Hunter Steele; to Peter Finch for reading the poetry section; Janet Hurrell for checking the bit on broadcasting; Dennis Pilling for sections referring to the British Library; and Mark Bide for putting up with my simplifications on metadata. Thanks also to Heather Rosenblatt, legal adviser to ALCS, for checking the sections on rights, and any errors that crept in after she read it are entirely my own. All of them helped me to make it a better book – and different readers would have made it a different better book.

I am grateful to individuals on the Writing and Computers forum who sent me their favourite Internet addresses, to Silent Three members who did the same, to all the colleagues of Colin Greenwood who responded with science fiction and fantasy sites of all kinds, and to many people everywhere who added to this cornucopia of writers' resources and corresponded with me about it. All email quotations within the text are quoted with permission.

Final thanks to Hazel Bell for doing the index and to Deborah Moggach for writing the Foreword.

The Publishers would like to thank the following for giving us permission to use material in the book:

Faber & Faber for lines from 'Choruses from "The Rock"' from *Collected Poems from 1909-1962* by T S Eliot (p. 140)

John Rudy Photography for the picture of Everybook's EB Dedicated Reader™ (p. 82)

Screen shots reprinted by permission from Microsoft Corporation.

Part 1

Introduction

Only connect

'Only connect,' E M Forster famously wrote. Perhaps that should now be, 'Only interconnect.' Linking to the Internet is part of what being a writer is today – joining an invaluable communications network. 'But is it invaluable? Isn't it a waste of time?' I hear you ask. I hope to answer that.

Forster's 'only connect' arose out of a supreme preoccupation with human connection in its moral and social aspects. Like many authors today, he was deeply suspicious of the technology of connectivity while having an uncanny ability to predict exactly how it would develop. His short story 'The Machine Stops' essentially anticipates the Internet and his warnings about how his imagined world might affect relationships, communities and their interconnections are as fresh now as they were in 1909 when the story was first published. The world needs writers like Forster as seers and thinkers to help make sense of this extraordinary development in modern society. If writers interconnect, become a part of the Internet, they will not only benefit from its assets but also free the imagination to construct stories about its future.

There are people who become addicted to it; their real lives devolve into virtual ones and they relate better in a world where silent and sometimes fantasy communication protects their identity.

So although it's good to connect, let's remember to disconnect as well, switch off the machines, listen to the flow and ebb of life around us. Communication and research via the Internet is astonishing, but it is not the only way of doing things. It does not *replace* the post, the telephone, going into libraries, browsing in bookshops, attending literary events or talking to people face-to-face. It is *as well as*. For a rich and varied life, writers, like everyone else, need a wide range of possibilities.

Why go online?

Your connectivity will depend only on your own need. Any of the following reasons will make joining the Net worthwhile:

- To use it as an extension of post and telephone
- To join writers' circles, genre writing societies, reading groups or authors' fan-clubs
- To locate agents, editors, translators or publishers
- To find books and bibliographical references
- For background research
- Because it makes co-authorship easier
- To extend writing opportunities into new art forms
- To resource those who teach on creative-writing courses
- For non-writerly reasons like ordering cheaper air tickets, finding out What's On, updating a Stock Market portfolio, finding medical information or Internet banking

The worries

- Becoming bombarded with email
- There's too much stuff and too much rubbish on the web
- Uncertainties about trusting information online
- Anxieties that you can't control copyright
- Privacy and security issues
- Catching viruses
- Detrimental effect on health
- Wasting time

This isn't a recipe book

This book explores the pros and cons listed in the boxed-out section above. It will not take you step-by-step through the processes of setting up your computer to connect to the Internet. Nor will it tell you how to dial in and what buttons to press when you get there. There are other books for that; this book is *specifically* for writers.

So if you want something that makes no assumptions *at all*, put this book down now and take it up again when you are ready to explore what the Internet can do for *you* as a *writer*.

If you want some of the basics explained in a way that has writers' interests in mind, then start at 'Getting connected' in Chapter 1. If you are already connected, skip straight to Chapter 2.

This *is* a cookbook

What's the difference? A recipe book describes exactly what ingredients to use and how to combine them. A cookbook gives the general principles together with tips and examples from personal experience.

I'll be giving a writer's-eye-view intermixed with personal comment. I'll say what I think is useful to writers and what is not. I indicate where I have uncertainties or prejudices and everyone can explore further by following the links at the back of the book.

My intention is to address all writers, regardless of genre or discipline. Perhaps you are browsing to see whether there are new outlets for traditional skills. Or perhaps you are looking to the Internet for totally new forms of creativity. Or you may be a part-time writer looking for advice and markets.

The concept of a 'writer' in itself needs re-examination, because words are no longer the only 'units' with which a modern author can work. Some of the people reading this might construct code, or imagine and create virtual spaces – such as film or animation scenarios – and have a non-verbal way of expressing them. Writing in words, sentences and format structures is no longer the only way of being creative with stories or ideas.

So I hope this book allows a broad interpretation of what it is to be a writer. Most of the principles and practical suggestions are independent of specifics, but occasionally – where there are common problems – I do whisper a bracketed aside.

I am not a seer, however. This is such a fast-moving area that even principles can change – a tiny stone thrown in a pond can have rippling consequences.

Why isn't this book online?

Everyone has been asking me this, as if the subject matter makes traditional publishing paradoxical. A full answer will emerge as the book progresses – it is, after all, a narrative with a structure. The short answer is that I believe in books. I believe in the traditional publishing values of editing and design. And I believe in the easy readability of black ink on crisp white paper.

It is a misunderstanding of what the Internet offers to presume that digital publishing replaces all forms of paper publishing. For some purposes it is preferable – for certain academic papers; for business information journals; for disposable literature (timetables, press releases, news sheets). But that is because it is such a good delivery mechanism that information can always be up to date. The Internet is *only* a delivery mechanism; *only* a connection between points.

A book has its own internal cohesion and even if readers dip about and read it in any order, there is still an intention behind the way it is constructed and the way its look-and-feel reflects that intention. Attempts to replicate the physicality of books have not yet been successful (though see the section on electronic books on page 74).

But there is something else too. You *can* find whole books on the Internet. You can certainly find mountains of essays, pamphlets and papers. It's easy to print them off or save them on disk to read on screen. The level of trust afforded is in proportion to the reader's perception of where they have come from. But in my experience they are almost always only of temporary value, and most of the time they get filed away unread (and lost to view if filed on disk). The Internet fosters a 'grab-it-while-you-can' mentality. Just in case. The result is a collection of look-alikes – from your own printer or your own screen; black-and-white noise that the mind can't cope with and therefore tends to ignore.

There's an economic argument in favour of traditional books, though I am confident that micropayment systems will soon make the economics of Internet publishing viable both for authors and publishers (see page 132). All the same, the Internet is a diffuse medium – it's all too easy to lose your readers as they click to another page. There's nothing wrong with that *per se*, but as a writer and a reader I favour the unity of a book.

I recognise that we all operate on two levels – how, as writers, we can make use of the Internet and how, as users, we can make *it* work for us. These two aims are not always compatible. For example, if I tantalised you above with a glimpse at Forster's story 'The Machine Stops', you might want to read it now, this minute. And you can if you're on the Internet because it's at http://www.plexus.org/forster/forster.html, but you will be breaking the law if you bring it to screen, save it or print it because it is in copyright and almost certainly illegally reproduced. It may even have gone 'off air' in response to a querying email. The point is, for a consumer and user this facility for instant gratification is a boon; but for writers with nothing to sell except their copyrights, the potential for being ripped off is an anxiety.

And, of course, some of this book *is* on the Internet – the bit you really want there, the chapter-by-chapter resource listing in Part 2 with live links is at http://www.internetwriter.co.uk. The password is *qixotica*. By the time you have finished reading, you will know how to expand the book for your own requirements. It is a hypertext book that reaches beyond itself to all the resources of the Internet.

1

Getting connected

You can define a net in one of two ways, depending on your point of view. Normally, you would say that it is a meshed instrument designed to catch fish. But you could, with no great injury to logic, reverse the image and define a net as a jocular lexicographer once did: he called it a collection of holes tied together with string.

Julian Barnes, *Flaubert's Parrot*

Can writers ignore the Internet?

You can write a novel, short story, poem or textbook without being wired up to the networks transmitting digital material all over the world. But you can also write without resort to a telephone. The trouble is, people who do not have telephones these days are considered to be out of touch. That is increasingly true of the Internet. Contact with co-authors, publishers and readers has never been easier. Dialling up information is quicker and cheaper than going to a library. There's little doubt that those who already have the computer equipment for word-processing, etc. can save time and costs by taking the further step of connecting to the Internet.

It isn't really necessary to know the mechanics of the Internet as long as you can switch on and dial up. After all, one isn't troubled by not knowing much about how cars or telephones work. As time goes on, it is becoming less and less necessary to learn the language of computers because strenuous attempts are being made to make using them intuitive. All the same, a few things need putting in context.

What is the Internet?

The Internet – or Net for short – is a distribution mechanism and a presentation device. It delivers content and acts as a medium through which anything can be bought and sold. It is also a proscenium arch through which performances of various kinds can be viewed. The arch, of course, is the screen; the performance, a way of displaying things we've hitherto had on paper, film or airwaves. Both roles interest the writer; the presentation role being perhaps the more challenging one.

Internet is an umbrella term to ascribe a structure to a complex system of hundreds of millions of computers in homes, offices and public buildings connected via telephone cabling. It is a net, or network, of laid lines or satellite-beamed signals with nodes (like the knots in a net) representing a sending machine and a receiving machine. The Internet is sometimes described as a Superhighway. It's not that, rather it is the roadways and intersections that cut across countries and continents, making it possible for people to get to each other.

To cut a well-worn story short, it began as an 'internetting' project to make computer-to-computer communication cheap. The world is fortunate that *de facto* standards evolved and came about soon after the Internet widened out from its first limited beginnings to commercial usage. It was quite unlike anything else that had preceded it in terms of standardisation amongst computers. It meant that anyone could communicate with anyone else.

The basis of this is a unified global addressing system known as Internet Protocol (IP). TCP/IP stands for Transmission Control Protocol/Internet Protocol. Broadly, TCP handles the delivery of messages and IP the network addressing.

Before that, we all had to agree about the way in which the transfer was made. It was like sending someone a letter to tell them that you were going to telephone and so agree to set up the telephone at a specific time so all the tuning devices (voltage, number of digits in a phone number, etc.) were at the same levels. Think what a mess we'd be in if we had to do that. Fortunately, the Consultative Committee for International Telephony and Telegraphy soon evolved, ensuring that telephone systems throughout the world can dial each other using an agreed numbering scheme and can recognise each other's dial tones and busy tones. We don't think about such things in relation to telephones and there is no longer any need to think about computer linking either. This ease of joining together probably accounts for the Internet's spectacular growth.

Main areas

If the Internet is the overall structure, what then are the main areas? To some extent this is not a relevant question because it is the doorway to anything you and the computer and the telephone line can do. But people puzzle over what they get, so, for clarification, a connection to the Internet provides four basic services:

Email	Chapter 2
World Wide Web	Chapter 3
Newsgroups	Chapter 4
Chat	Chapter 4

You can use all or some of these and you can have some of them disabled or restricted. Some people may identify other services as being basic, but the above four are the ones that matter to writers.

Digital form

The Internet works because it is able to translate all types of creative activity and communication into digital form.

Digital (as opposed to analogue) means representing information as numbers with fixed values. It may help to imagine this by comparing the digital clock (discrete changes of display) with the analogue or traditional clock (continuous variation). The computer stores the actual words on the page in discrete digits. Computers can only handle information once it has been expressed as numbers.

Thoughts and expressions are reduced to a series of on/off switches – either a 0 or a 1. This is the underlying particle of digital computing and is called a bit. Music, art-work, video, sound and the written word all reduce to a series of bits. A string of 8 bits is called a byte and represents a single letter, number or symbol of the alphabet.

Imagine the 0s to be white and the 1s to be black – then everything in between consists of fine gradations of shades of grey. The same goes for loud and soft. These crude examples are helpful for visualising what's going on – showing that digitality is what translates *all* media into a form that can be understood by and transmitted by the Internet. Nicholas Negroponte, guru of MIT (the Media Lab at Massachusetts Institute of Technology) describes digitality as the DNA of information.

The equipment

Satellite connection through a television set will soon be enough. For now a PC or Macintosh computer, not more than five years old, is best. If it did not come fitted with a modem (see below), buy one.

Obviously, we all need an Internet Service Provider (known as an ISP), which is the company that connects us to the networks. So-called 'free' service providers offering email and web space are springing up everywhere. How free these will prove to be is uncertain (see below).

In addition, the UK government is committed to giving every school child over the age of nine a free email address and free web space for life by the year 2002. Access in school will be free – financially speaking – but whether it will be freely available is anybody's guess. Pledges to wire every family into the Internet by way of their children are politically astute, but the reality may well turn out to be less exciting than the smooth talk. Don't expect this to provide a way in for you and your family. It's a bit like giving everyone the bicycle key when the cycle itself doesn't have two wheels.

The lubricating oil will be software that is destined to provide the 'how' of all this interconnection. I have seen the alpha-test software for an educational product that the government has heralded, and there is little doubt that it will radically alter learning and communication methodologies. Obviously that is going to have a knock-on effect in the commercial world. It also means that committed parents will need to keep up. At the moment that means getting the kit at home.

Modem

This is an internal or external device that connects the computer to other computers through the telephone wires. The word comes from an elision of MOdulator and DEModulator. The modem carries digital bits down the telephone lines. These are whistling tones – lower tones for a 0 and slightly higher tones for a 1. That's why you hear squeaky noises from computer modems (and fax machines) as they connect. Once you get into dedicated lines, the oscillations work at millions per second and you can't hear the squeaks.

An external modem is easier to fit, though an internal card modem might be cheaper. It is a false economy to get anything less than the fastest in the shop. A dedicated ISDN (Integrated Services Digital Network) line is only worth it if there's a special offer as it is only two to four times faster than a 56K modem, currently the standard. I'd wait and watch for ADSL (Asymmetrical Digital Subscriber Line) which is a broadband connection that is 15 times faster – it squeezes up to 99 per cent more capacity out of a phone line without interfering with your regular phone services. That means you could be simultaneously talking on the phone or sending a fax and be connected to the Internet at the same time. If all goes according to plan, that includes continuous connection to the Internet for a probable monthly charge of £35–£45. Whatever the tariff, any ADSL deployment will take years to complete and may not reach the whole of the UK.

Meanwhile modems are stuck with baud rates. Baud is a word borrowed from telegraphy to describe measuring the rate at which information can travel. The baud rate is taken as meaning the number of bits per second (bps) that can be transmitted. A standard 56K modem (56,000 bps) should transmit about 1000 words in one second, though, in practice, it depends on your telephone connection.

In sharing information via a computer and telephone network, the receiving machine has to co-operate with the sending – or host – machine. This is sometimes called handshaking. The co-operation expresses itself in the form of agreements about the way in which the transfer is being made – the speed, 'stop bits', parity and so on. With the current breed of plug-and-play modems and software wizards (easy set-up guides), it shouldn't be necessary to get involved in the ins and outs of how this is done (or the protocols, to use the jargon). But if something goes wrong, it's as well to know some of the terminology so that you can talk to the whizz-kids on the help-line.

Fax

An added perk of being connected to the Internet is that it can replace a dedicated fax machine – in a limping sort of way. It works by modem through the computer. Power has to be on and the computer must be set to send or receive faxes, which can be a bind. A fax is 'read-only' because it is a picture of the page and therefore slower to send than an equivalent amount of text as an email. Because it is a picture (or rather a bit-map) the text can't be altered.

Those who want to fax pictures or diagrams could consider getting a scanner rather than a fax machine. They're generally cheaper and have other uses too – for pictures and graphics and also as primitive, but adequate, photocopiers. Faxing like this is not ideal, but email has so surpassed fax for text exchange that the occasions on which a writer might want to send a fax are diminishing.

Telephone networks

As stated above, the telephony agreements ensure compatibility throughout the world so it does not matter what phone line you use.

Internet calls are almost universally charged at a local rate, so whether you are sending emails to California or Russia or Chile it would still only be the cost of a single local call. Note, though, that the fabled 1p a minute is (at the time of writing) subject to a 4.7p minimum charge at any time of day. That allows roughly 1 minute during the working week and 4½ minutes at weekends (though cable companies are getting more competitive). The call charge starts when you hear the whistling tone so if you have a slow connection, or if your free ISP constantly fails to connect you, the costs can mount up.

My personal view is that the Internet will not fully flower in the UK until telecom companies offer hours rather than minutes of telephone time for the cost of one call. The freelance writer working at home needs such access because so many research possibilities are easily available. And even though it saves time and Tube fares, most people will be anxious about the amount of telephone time that is clocking up. And it *does* mount up. There is a glimmering on the horizon – ISPs that offer evening and weekend connections free, or for 6.5p per call regardless of duration, and a suggestion that some might use 0800 numbers. I doubt if we'll be able to stay online all day – as people can in the US and Australia, but call-inclusive subscriptions are on the way. The Free the Net campaign is moving fast.

The British government has not so far accepted that Internet access is not reaching its potential because of call charges though there are signs that it is beginning to look favourably on the Campaign for Unmetered Telecommunications (CUT). Although ADSL (and other broadband Internet access services) may effectively allow unmetered cable connection, many individuals will not be willing to pay the tariff or able to get the service, so although the signs are looking hopeful, we are not out of the woods yet.

The service provider

I don't want to survey the whole range of Internet Service Providers (ISPs), but if you want Mercedes Benz reliability Demon and Pipex have consistently been among the best and Pipex provides backbone services to companies such as Reuters that *require* guaranteed access.

If that isn't an issue, then some research is necessary. Internet magazines have top-ten listings. It's surprising how many of them there are and equally surprising that different ISPs get to the top of the listing each month. These are companies that offer you, the individual, a gateway to the Internet – some are free, some charge (see below). They usually provide their own software (or buy in a known brand) and they may support other brands. The criteria you might want to think about when choosing an ISP are:

- Do they have a good reputation? Ask friends if they can get online first time, every time.
- What is the software like and how easy is it to use one of the industry-standard mailing programs instead?
- What is the support like – try ringing the support line and see how quickly they answer and how friendly they are. And does it cost extra?
- How easy is it to send large files as attachments? (Vital for authors, this one – more detail below.) Does the attachment come as one long file in one mailing, or will it break it up into 16 (or so) different packets, thus making it alarming for the person receiving it at the other end?
- Has the ISP got enough bandwidth, or are there going to be bottle-necks and engaged signals at busy times of the day? Remember that the bulk of Internet users are still in the US, so the busy times of day are trans-America business hours.
- Does the ISP force you to start browsing the Internet from its own front pages so that you might get annoyed by lots of advertising?

- Does the ISP allow unlimited connection time for a fixed fee or do you at a certain point have to pay extra? Once you start using the web (see Chapter 3) a few hours a month will not be enough and the charges will mount up.
- Are you trying out a free month on a CD-ROM that came with a magazine or bundled with your computer when you bought it (most likely AOL or CompuServe)? If so, then don't feel you have to stick with it. Don't give out a temporary email address to all your friends, because you might then feel 'stepp'd in so far' and stick with the supplier just in order to keep things simple.
- How free are the free ISPs?
- What is the address (see page 19) and do you like it; e.g. jane.dorner@screaming.net doesn't appeal even if it gives free connection at weekends.

How free is free?

So far there's always been a catch such as charging 50p to £1 a minute for support, use of irritating advertising and not enough bandwidth to satisfy all the customers. Free ISPs usually have to pay a telecoms company for bandwidth and the only way they can recoup that expense is by keeping you online as long as possible because they, in turn, receive a percentage of the cost of the call. So if access is slow, you'll have to stay online longer. Or if you dial through, but fail to log on because they're overloaded, it still costs 5p; the free ISP doesn't care because it is making a profit from that call and it isn't offering quality service, it is offering a free service – for which you are actually paying.

Paying a rental fee (typically £10–15 a month) will guarantee reliability and added-value services.

Email abroad

People who travel a lot and need to be in contact, will want to choose a provider with an 0800 number, a list of local numbers abroad or a 'roaming service' – you'll presumably have a laptop with a modem to plug into the venue abroad. CompuServe and AOL are good abroad and many people choose them for that reason. Telephone your service provider and ask for details of emailing from abroad: there's often a premium to pay.

Some providers also have web-browser-based access to a pass-word-protected email box and that is quite useful for picking up mail if you can get local access from someone else's line, in a cyber-café or a library or at a friend's. Free services like Hotmail and Delphi also allow travelling access from the web.

Email software

There are some market leaders and any self-respecting ISP will offer at least some minimal hints on how to set up your machine for email software other than the one that comes as part of the basic package. Market leaders have for some years been Eudora, Pegasus, Netscape and Outlook; there are other good programs, but I've always been in favour of the big names because you can get support and help from colleagues and you know that the company will continue to produce upgrades.

Setting up the software for your email address (or for more than one) is not transparently self-evident. Take some time to do it slowly – follow every move in the printed instructions or use a soft-ware tutorial wizard if you possibly can. And when it is working, copy down all the settings in the 'customise', 'options' or 'tools'

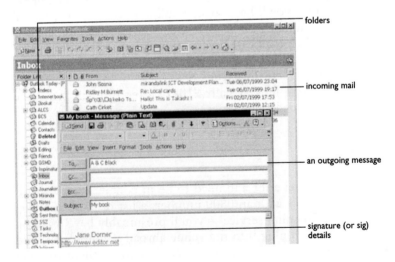

Microsoft Outlook email environment

pop-up boxes so that if anything goes wrong you can set it up again easily. Write the setting details on a piece of paper together with your password and user name (which may be a numeral) and keep it *safe*.

You dial in to the Internet either from your email program or from your web browser. The same dial-up setting will work with both – though you may have to choose whether you want the program to dial in as soon as you load it or only on demand. I suggest the latter, so you keep control. You can also set an email program to dial in automatically every hour, or twice a day, or at any specified interval. People in business seem to like this, but writers concentrating on a text may find it an intrusion. The whole joy of email is surely that it is not like the jangling telephone that demandingly interrupts your flow of thought, yet the immediacy of contact can be there if you want it.

For more detail on how writers can benefit most from email, go to Chapter 2, page 19.

Browsers

You access the Internet via a program known as a browser – (e.g. Netscape, Internet Explorer and the newer Opera). The browser can double up as an email program, and act as the centre of all your connectivity, but many people have a dedicated email program for correspondence and use the browser for connecting to the web. The browser should be set up so that it dials the connecting phone number when you have selected an address.

This is what all the bits of the browser are for:

The Microsoft Internet Explorer browser

Browsers work because links are embedded into documents using HTML (HyperText Mark-up Language). Anything so coded can link with any other document anywhere in the world, no matter where it is stored. The user doesn't see any of this coding but moves through 'pages' of information by clicking a pointer device on a prompt word – or hyperlink – (traditionally an underlined phrase appearing on-screen in blue). These links are coded instructions to your computer to go and fetch a page from another address. A 'page' can be of variable length; generally half to three printed A4 pages, but it can be 20. Hyperlinking is explained in more detail on page 36.

Although people often think computers are complicated, conceptually something very simple is going on when you click your mouse over a hyperlink. The browser program sends a message across the Internet requesting information from another program (known as a server) running on a computer somewhere else in the world. The server sends back a message containing the information. It's no more incomprehensible than telephony.

The address is called a Uniform Resource Locator (URL) and starts with the prefix 'http://'. That is just a simple bit of code that switches in to HyperText Transfer Protocol. The next bit is generally (but not always) 'www', short for World Wide Web. Then comes the domain name. The domain is a unique Internet address labelled by a name, which could be 'yourname' and then the identifying part of the domain – whether it's a company 'co', an organisation 'org' or a commercial enterprise 'com' and which part of the world the domain is in; 'com' and 'net' can be anywhere (but mostly US), 'uk' is Britain, 'ie' is Ireland, 'jp' is Japan and so on. This address name is used for the web address (after http://www.) as well as the email address (the part after the @ sign).

Browsing

In its computer sense, browsing describes a way of flicking through screens of information and is not unlike browsing through a book. The difference is that everything looks the same on screen, so that if you are looking something up – in your own text files, in the computer's help system or in an electronic information store – there will be no visual clues to help you find the same bit of information again (position on the page, coffee-stain, turned down corner, etc.). In addition, extended reading is not yet comfortable on screens and although this may change in the future, it looks as if browsing through large amounts of text is still more popularly done on paper.

Page

The people responsible for popularising the language of the Internet still refer to the text and graphics that show at any one time in a browser as a 'page'. It isn't, of course. It can be anything from one paragraph to the equivalent of 10 printed pages (rarely more) but you only see the bit framed by your screen at any one time. That's why the browser has what's called a scroll bar on the right-hand side, so you can move the screen frame down the 'page'. We're returning, in a sense, to the Chinese scroll.

Document

Long screeds on the web are still referred to as a 'document'. Odd, that. It used to describe an important paper or papers, often with a legal resonance, at least instructional (after all, it comes from 'docere', meaning 'to teach'). Now it means any facsimile of meaningful data that can be in printed or electronic form.

Perhaps it is useful to have a generic term for all types of written material. Many word-processing programs seem to accept this by automatically stamping filenames with a DOC extension (formatted and known as a document file) and TXT (no formatting and known as a text file). They do not all do this, of course, but it is a useful convention for distinguishing between different types of computer files.

You may also come across documents with the extension PDF, short for Portable Document Format, which is a universal standard for preserving the original appearance – fonts, formatting, colours and graphics – of any source document, regardless of the application and platform used to create it. PDF files are compressed, which means they are smaller than the originals and therefore travel down the phone lines faster, making them of particular importance to writers on the Internet. See Chapter 3, page 54 for details on PDF.

Going online without owning a computer

Once upon a time there used to be a hatter's at every street corner. Now there's the cybercafé or mailbox booth. In some cities 'culture centres', which have banks of computers *inter alia*, are replacing public libraries. All allow you to rent computer facilities by the hour (some may be free), either just for surfing the Internet or also including a password-locked mailbox of your own. Some public libraries also offer browsing facilities for online research.

The advantage of renting time to dip a toe in the water is that there is no need for any capital outlay before being sure the Internet has something to offer. It can help build confidence for the technophobe. Internet cafés are friendly places where others sit with a cup of coffee and someone will always help. You'll find a database of cafés all over the world in the listing in Part 2:1 **Internet culture**, page 161, as well as libraries in the UK offering access. Get a friend to print out the listings.

The comforting thing about computing – online or off-line – is that those who *can* love helping those who *can't*. It is a tremendous democratising agent – we're all novices here; some more or less so. There's constant reciprocity in know-how, at any level.

Computers, being machines, are inherently counter-intuitive mechanisms. There is a pleasure to be derived from beating the system, as it were. It appeals to the crossword-puzzle gene in all of us – if you can work out what the rule is, you can solve the clue. And the original historical clue was the ball of twine that Theseus used to find his way out of the Labyrinth. Which brings us neatly back to the idea of a net or network and to the quote with which this chapter began.

Resources for Chapter 1 in Part 2 and online

2

Email

'Watson, come here; I want you.'

The first complete sentence Alexander Graham Bell
transmitted by telephone, 10 March 1876

Email offers the most obvious benefits to writers. It is much
cheaper than either post or telephone and is the fastest way of
delivering copy. The mechanics of getting connected were
described in Chapter 1; now for what happens after that.

Writing phone calls

The mailing program is a notepad unit for creating, sending and
filing messages – it usually holds finished messages in a queue
waiting to be transmitted when you next dial in to your service
provider. Your incoming post is dumped into the mailbox for
viewing when you come off-line – this is so that you do not waste
telephone time reading or writing emails. Remember that when
you press a button marked 'Send' it may go into your outbox until
you next dial in. It's like putting it in a postbox, except that you
decide on collection times yourself.

Technology is unforgiving: the address has to be absolutely
correct. The @ sign in the address joins your unique identifier
(which may be your name) with the service provider's address. The
dots in the address separate the different parts of it and are
important – your mail would be returned to you if you used
commas instead of dots. So 'co.uk' is a UK company; 'ac.uk'
signifies 'academic'; 'com' means commercial; and so on. It is worth
understanding what the codes stand for as they give clues about
who your correspondent is. Email addresses are normally written
in lower case.

You can have several different mailboxes on one machine and

each one is password-protected so no-one else can read your mail if you do not want them to. It can be useful to have different mailbox identities so, if your service provider gives you five boxes, consider before parcelling them out to your family. You might want one in a pen name, for example, or you might want one for receiving material from special interest groups or mailing lists so that the flow does not interrupt your everyday mail. Of course, a sophisticated mailing program allows you to sort incoming mail directly into different boxes, but the outgoing signature (i.e. your own email address) remains the same.

Advantages

The joy of email is that it is instant, but also unobtrusive. And cheap. So you can contact one, two or several hundred people with a single phone connection. Quite often the reply is waiting for you when you next log on – this is most useful for connections abroad. The etiquette (known as netiquette) is to reply briefly and quickly. There's no need to waste time in letter-writing niceties; it's fine to plunge straight in to the matter in hand, copying the relevant bit of the message back to the person you are answering so they have a record of what they said together with the specific point you are answering. This is useful – some people have a habit of sending a reply with an unadorned 'yes' (or 'no') and one's often forgotten what was asked.

It is also good practice to keep messages short, with single subject themes per message (i.e. send five clearly subject-labelled emails if you have five different things to say). That way both of you can keep track of subject themes and can retain the to-and-fro of correspondence on a single topic with ease. This can prove extremely useful in cases of misunderstanding or dispute, e.g. when exactly did an editor commission a piece from you and what precisely was the brief. Some people print out emails to keep track of what was said. I file mine electronically, but that's a choice to suit each individual. Most writers tend to feel safer with paper copies.

Expressivity is added by using non-alphabetic keys. A word is enclosed in asterisks to indicate *emphasis* (don't use caps because it looks like SHOUTING). Or there are 'emoticons' like a colon, hyphen and close bracket :-) to represent a smile; some people put <grin> to indicate friendliness or irony, but mercifully this brand of twee-ness is now going out of fashion.

There is also a level of flippancy in email that has become acceptable discourse, enabling helpful informality. Many people consider this a culturally interesting development and useful in our communication-intensive age. Postgraduate theses are being written on the phenomenon.

Email is essential for some writing genres and a significant time-saver for others. Journalists, for example, increasingly rely on email to file copy especially if they are communicating from abroad. Newspaper and magazine editors also prefer to receive copy by email because they can then bring it into their own word-processor to mark up rather than have it retyped or wait for the disk to arrive. If you are a Graham Greene, you can submit work in pencil, but for most people the easier you make the editor's life, the easier it will be for your work to be accepted. Book editors, on the other hand, will not welcome receipt of a manuscript by email, especially without any prior discussion. See **Submitting work to publishers** on page 25.

Disadvantages

These are slight. It's very rare to catch a virus from an email because viruses usually occur in program files. So if someone unknown sends you a program (ending .EXE) as an attachment, you'll generally be safe if you do not open it. See pages 58–9 for more on viruses.

Another worry is junk mail (see below). This is unlikely to be acute unless you advertise. Some people send more trivial communications than are strictly necessary, but you can deal with them briefly and the corollary is that friends and relatives abroad are delightfully accessible.

Another disadvantage is that relationships with people who never meet and never talk seem somehow unreal and perhaps they won't last unless reinforced by a genuine encounter at some point.

Talking email

Voice email is a relative newcomer and awaits the broadband connection revolution; a voice email audio clip is slower to send. However, digital audio compression technology is getting better. You can say quite a lot in a 25-second voice email and it compresses down to about 20K, which is not a lot, and apparently one speaks at 250 words a minute and types at 50, so there is some time-saving potential there. The program I used let me add a little picture of myself so the recipient can see who's talking (Eudora, which has a voice plug-in, does not have that facility). It takes a little longer in telephone penny-a-minute time, but for those who feel at home with dictation, or who can talk better than they write, or who want their enthusiasm, despair or friendship to show in the tone of voice, this is an interesting novelty. I think it will catch on. It could be the answer to Repetitive Strain Injury anxieties, but the voice emailing systems are still in their infancy.

Is email secure?

Yes, and no. Sending an email is like sending an open postcard. Theoretically anyone could read it – not just the postman. But they would have to have a van in the neighbourhood intercepting signals that they could then capture and decode. A devoted hacker can find a way of reading your mail – but so could they in any other form of communication. If there's no reason why they should bother, then it probably won't happen. Once someone has collected email, it is no longer on the ISP's mail server. See also page 130 for safety of sending credit card details by email.

Plain text

Email messages are usually in plain text because computers can only share information by converting letters to numbers. ASCII is an acronym (now almost a word and pronounced 'ass-kee') standing for the numbering system: American Standard Code for Information Interchange. It's a bit of jargon you can't do without. Converting to ASCII is supposed to be the *lingua franca* of computers; the theory being that giving every letter and character a numerical value which is common to all word-processors of all kinds will mean that they can all share text files. Such files are called plain text or straight text or non-document text – so no icing like italics, bold and so on.

In general it is best to set your email settings to send in plain text, rather than HTML format, because it loads faster – there will be a choice in the Options or Tools menus of the email program.

A little tip for Word users (97 and later) – if your co-author sends you text in the body of an email message, then you can block copy it into a Word document, but it will (annoyingly) have soft line endings at the ends of each line. To remove them, go to the Format Menu, select AutoFormat and then in the drop-down box you'll see a little arrow beside the rubric 'General document'. Click that and select Email; then OK it. Magic. That solution came to me by email in a monthly e-zine (electronic magazine) called WordTips http://www.VitalNews.com – and it's a small irritation so easily solved.

In case anyone thinks I'm pro Word, it's true I use it for compatibility's sake, but lots of writers prefer WordPro (PC), Nisus (Mac), WordPerfect (both) and the DOS Protext.

Parcel posting: attachment files

When fax came in, some of us agonised about what to say on the cover sheet. It wasn't logical to say 'I attach', or 'I enclose' so we coined 'I affax' or 'I append'. Email solves this by offering a little icon, which indicates that a file is attached. Attachments (also called enclosures) are truly one of the miracles of modern technology. And I *do mean* modern. It's no good stumbling on with version 2 of a word-processing program if most colleagues are on version 8.

An email is more like a memo than a letter, but the medium is also ideal for transmitting longer documents. Anything that goes into several pages, or relies to some extent on layout (even if it is just italicisation), is best sent as an attachment. Most mailer programs display a paperclip or clothespeg icon; double click to attach a word-processed file to the message. Anything electronic can be so attached – a desk-top published file, digital pictures, even music. It takes much longer to send (and receive) than a plain text email, but it is still cheaper than paper, envelopes and postage stamps. And immediate. This book, for example, is about 1 Mb in size and it would take the current BT minimum rate of 4.7p of telephone time to send it. Generally speaking it will arrive in your co-author or publisher's mailbox within a quarter of an hour (large files sometimes get stuck in a queuing system at busy times). The advantages of that hardly need spelling out.

If speed is important, I'd want to do a test run first because not all programs handle attachments in the same way. Although I know that I can exchange large files without problem, not everyone can. You might have to break a book up into chapters and send them one at a time.

Sending or receiving an attachment can be alarming at first. If it doesn't work as described in the next paragraph, then tinker with the set-up options to make sure the settings are right.

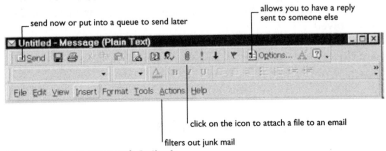

The email bar in Microsoft Outlook

Click on the icon (or it may just say 'Attach'), select the file you want to attach from a drop-down box, double click and a document icon with the filename should appear in your message. Press Send. You've been to the post office and back – your manuscript has gone to your editor or co-author and you haven't even had to wrap it up, lick the stamp or queue up to record it. At the other end, the recipient double clicks on the icon in the email message and the document opens up in whatever word-processor is associated with it.

It's magical and on an imaginary writer's Internet desert island, you would take with you the ability to send email with attachment files. But there's a complication (of course there is; this is computing) the sender and the recipient must have compatible equipment. Plain text (or ASCII, see above) is all very well, but useless for a two-column drama layout or anything relying on formatting.

Try doing these things in the following order:

- First make sure that the types of files you are using are associated with a particular software program, e.g. that a DOC file opens in Word or WordPerfect (should be automatic or try the Open With command in Windows Explorer).

- Save the file as RTF (Rich Text Format) as well as in your normal document format and send both.
- Find out what program or what *version* of the same program your partner has and save your file in that format before sending. E.g. if you have upgraded to Word 2000 and the other person has Word 6 or lower then you must save it down in the older format.
- If communicating between a Mac and a PC, do a trial run first. There isn't space here to enumerate the pitfalls as it depends which programs both of you are using. If the Mac adds an extension name that the PC can't understand (BIN or DAT) then the chances are the sender has sent it in 8-bit binary rather than in Mime. Don't bother about the jargon here, just ask them to send it again in Mime (choosable from an Options menu). You can sometimes save the situation by changing the filename, but it's far from plain sailing even when both parties are using the same version of Word. Sometimes the problem is caused by people using an unusual font that the person at the receiving end does not have – if in doubt, use Times Roman or Arial.
- If you find you can only send it as a TXT file then do some searching and replacing first. E.g. convert all the italics to phrases enclosed by asterisks – a quick search and replace at the other end converts them back. The same can be done with tabs, but it's less reliable.
- If you receive an attachment file, remember where you saved it to.

Submitting work to publishers

Although email exchange is useful for short submissions – and almost *de rigueur* in the newsprint world – a long work should always be printed out and delivered in the traditional manner.

As I said above, don't send a whole unsolicited manuscript to a publisher or an agent as an attachment. They generally prefer a traditional approach – explanatory letter, outline and specimen section. Many will be irritated and will not welcome another dollop on the electronic slush pile. Every editor knows how easy it is to send the same email to a dozen others and they'll suspect you of doing it. If you want the editor to think you're special, you must treat them as if they are special too.

Besides, for your own protection it is unwise to part with a complete easy-to-copy text until you have a contract with a publisher or script producer and an agreed method of document exchange. It does happen to writers that an idea or treatment they think is uniquely theirs is turned down and something very close to it appears a little later – more often in the film and TV world than in books. This happens for many genuine reasons; two people *do* think of identical plots and scenarios. It's as if there were some sort of morphic resonance; something in the communal air. The writer who feels hard done by, however, invariably suspects that their work has been kidnapped. Why put yourself at risk? It's far too easy for electronic works to be copied and manipulated (see **Plagiarism and manipulation**, page 146,) and until word-processors routinely provide watermarking identification associated with any paragraph, so that it carries its owner's identification tag even if it is cut and copied into someone else's text, it's wise to be protective of your own work.

Back to paper

You can only really see what you have written when it is printed out on paper. Some aficionados say that this is because a generation of writers reading from screens has not yet grown up. When they do, they will not only have overcome the disadvantages of screen readability (more on page 120), but will have the confidence that they can retrieve the thoughts and expressions that appear to be buried within the computer on other and invisible 'pages'.

Less experienced Internet users feel that whatever is not visible is somehow inaccessible. This clearly requires a restructuring of expectations. We have been used to looking at words on a page in order to read them. Now we have to get used to looking through screens to the words beyond. The pixellisation of thoughts into the dots and gaps which paint the words on-screen alters our view of what texts are.

So far, there has been a collective rejection of screen-reading (except for quick reference) hence an ongoing need for paper copies. Reasons include: the portability of paper, ease on the eye, poor graphic design for screens, the requirement for marginalia and tracking changes (only clumsily possible on screens), the tactility and movability of paper, and the peace and quiet away from the motor roar. Besides this, even seeing the text in a different form or shape induces a renewed perspective on its content. A writer may see more or less easily what changes to make if the words are transformed into one of a dozen pleasing or unpleasing typefaces. Even printing out a chapter at a shorter line length, or different spacing, gives the creative spirit room to play. All editors know that mistakes can be missed in typescript, but suddenly jump to the eye when the thing is printed – because of the easier readability of a properly typeset line. It's well known that proof-readers often spot mistakes in a script they have picked over as they put it upside-down into an envelope. So hard copy, paper copy, the print-out, the manuscript – whatever you call it – is always needed.

However expert one becomes at reading on-screen, the text looks different on paper. New points strike the reader or writer, typographical errors leap to the eye when displayed differently, something that looked cogent at 250 words to a screen, doesn't hold water as you flick through a sheaf of papers, and so on. One novelist of my acquaintance writes her novel on a word-processor and on final print-out she destroys all electronic versions. She then sits down with the script, edits it and types the whole thing out again. I couldn't do that myself, but I find it admirable: you'd be very alert to anything that wasn't working and very reluctant to type it out again.

For all these reasons, a paper copy should accompany book-length scripts submitted in an electronic version and this paper copy should be regarded as the definitive version in case of dispute. Subsequent alterations may be marked on it (but see **Document comparison** below). The paper copy must be identical to the electronic copy.

Co-authorship

Perhaps the pre-eminent new opportunity that email has presented to writers is the astonishing ease of co-authorship. There are two versions of this – collaboration for traditional publication and multi-authored online patchworks.

Traditional collaboration

Academic authors have always worked with other people in the same subject fields. In abstruse branches of science, for example, where everyone knows who the other experts across the world are, researchers tend to carve up the territory between themselves so that duplication of effort does not occur. Email has reduced what once took months to a few days.

In business, as well as academia, people are working together on the same projects and can integrate texts with consummate ease. Everyone still needs the red pencil at the ready, but there are now new ways of wielding it. Since textual exchange is electronic, it is hard for people to see what another author has done to alter the text, or how to comment upon it, unless everyone decides on a procedure before starting.

Codes of practice

It is not just how you and your co-author, editor or reader manage to read the files that matters, but also how you decide to deal with them. As this is electronic you will need to invent your own codes of practice because the paper paradigms do not apply.

Or do they? Copyright exists in electronic formats just as for paper ones. It's alarmingly easy to alter a colleague's electronic text without paying sufficient attention to the fact that it is not yours. Not only is integrity at stake, but colleagues need to know how their work has been edited. So try out tracking methods like these:

- Decide every time the MS changes hands who has the 'live master' copy and try to ensure that only one person is working on it at any given time.
- Use different screen text colours or highlighter markings for each person.
- Use the hidden 'sticky' notelet areas or comment boxes that up-to-date word-processors offer.
- Invent a creative use of the footnote function as an insertion point for a comment.
- Identify comment points with a bookmark and type the remarks separately.
- Contain comments or edited text within personal delimiters such as ### or [ ] or << >>.
- If editing an emailed excerpt, return the original and interrupt it with a double carriage return every time you are suggesting a change so the recipient can see where to pay attention.
- Use a document-comparison utility (see opposite).

It is wise to establish preferred roles before the writing starts in order to avoid misunderstandings later. Best also to thrash out matters of copyright ownership; equity of contribution and revision rights; division of royalties; order of title credits; and style of writing.

Even where people are collaborating on a writing project for which notions of ownership are peripheral, it is still a good idea to agree at the beginning on the way in which revisions will be done. It is tedious to read two versions line for line against each other.

Copyright in projects written by committee – or by several employees of a company – are owned by the commissioning body. Ease of alteration therefore becomes an advantage, whereas for private co-authors it is something of a threat. Industry already makes full use of collaborative tools: conferencing software for brainstorming sessions; corporate document structures and style rules available as computer templates; boilerplating techniques (i.e. movable standard paragraphs); networked file exchange; tailored grammar-checkers; interactive training. The more limited the subject material (technical, medical, legal, etc.) the easier it is for a company to devise systems to create uniformity (and hence safety) in its company documentation.

Document comparison

Author-editor and author-author interactions depend on each person being able to see what changes the other has made. On paper this is obvious; on screens it is not, but it is possible to trace editorial changes by overlaying one version on top of another. This is variously known as red lining, edit trace, track changes or document comparison and you'll probably find it in the Tools menu of your word-processor.

Document comparison can be done automatically by getting the computer to compare one version of a text against another. It does what computers are supposed to do: it saves time. The value is in being able to trace differences between two versions electronically and in seconds, rather than laboriously reading two texts line by line against each other.

Texts do not have to be written in the same word-processor though it's usually best if they are converted to the same format. Word-processors allow you to record all the changes between a new and an older version of a text – on Word it is in the Tools Menu in the Track Changes option. The user is then able to view all deletions, replacements, insertions and moved text and see exactly what changes have been made. This can be done by looking at the two side by side on a split screen, or as a composite print-out which shows each type of change in a different style, or as a comparison file back in the word-processor.

The user chooses display styles – e.g. crossed out red for deleted text; a grey shading for sections that have changed position; blue bold for new material; underline for formatting changes.

The version number

Plato is reputed to have redrafted the opening sentence of *The Republic* 50 times. Hemingway apparently rewrote the end of *Farewell to Arms* 49 times. Margaret Mitchell rewrote the beginning of *Gone with the Wind* 70 times. Such stories abound. Presumably, all but the published version were drafts.

Internet publication gives a new meaning to such 'drafting'. From the point of view of a literary scholar, it is a possible loss that we may not be able to look back at the workings of the genius mind and follow through the different drafts that led to the final copy unless the writer has saved every single version and, plainly, this is unlikely. Academics are already mourning the loss for researchers of the future.

One of the author's concerns is to keep track of different drafts and to ensure that early versions are not circulated where a new one has already replaced it. You can do this by keeping track of the dates of files, or by renaming them, but try not to let multiple revisions clutter up the folder. It's probably better to put draft1 or draft2 onto whatever archive medium you use (disk, zip drive or writable CD-ROM) clearly labelled, just in case you do want to return to it, but keep early versions off your working folder.

Multi-authoring

What I called multi-authoring patchworks come into Chapter 6, page 99. These are interactive texts involving people who write to a theme that is loosely woven together, or contribute to an ongoing saga, or take responsibility for a particular character in a 'cyber-soap'. Contributors write off-line and then email their section perhaps to a co-ordinator or maybe to all the participants. It's all very experimental and some writers find it absorbing.

Junk mail

Yes, it does exist. But you can choose to filter out anything you do not wish to receive. A good email program will allow you to select incoming email and add it to a junk list so you never receive anything from that source again. If not, then you may need to acquire something with the delightful name of a spammer slammer. 'Spam' is unsolicited commercial mail, and you get it all the time anyway. Don't reply to it, don't email back asking to be removed from the list (as that just confirms who you are). Get a junk-mail filter.

Or there's that interesting word 'munging' – you munge yourself from a bulk emailing by adding the word 'spamblock' after the '@' sign in any return address you give on a website. A human user will soon learn that you have to remove 'spamblock' in the reply, but automated email robots that collect up names from websites in order to send out advertising do not.

Cold calling

Journalists will know how enervating cold calling can be. You need to talk to an expert, get a quote or offer an idea for a piece. But the logistics of getting the right moment on the phone shorten the working day. First thing in the morning isn't good because the person you are calling is dealing with morning mail, isn't in yet or has meetings. Lunch times can go from 12 to 3.30. After lunch is bad if you're offering a story because busy editors are rushing to their own deadlines. It boils down to between 10.30 and 12 a.m. and then you might start up an answerphone to answerphone dialogue that gets embarrassing.

Email is less intrusive and in my experience editors do reply (if with brevity bordering on the peremptory). I've written articles as a result of 'cold emailing': it's as successful as any other approach from the cold. I think it helps if you have your own web pages so the editor can look you up and browse whatever else you've done. (See **Writing web pages**, page 113.)

Interviewing by email

A journalist friend who was not on the Internet once had to find six people to interview for an article: men who had not been present at the birth of their child but wished they had. She was ringing round all her friends to see if they knew anyone and it wasn't proving easy. So I said, Look, why don't I put up a note on a mailing list and see who comes forward. I found a parenting listserv (explained on page 69) and popped the question. Four men offered themselves, one in the UK (so she phoned him) and three in the US, so we devised an interview by email (it wasn't a glossy magazine with a large expense budget).

Email interviewing doesn't replace intuitively following your subject's lead and getting clues from tone of voice, but telephone interviewing was itself always a poor second to the face-to-face chat – though nevertheless a necessarily acquired skill in certain branches of journalism or even research for a book. You couldn't do a full-length profile this way, but it's ideal for the kind of article outlined above.

Advantages

There are advantages. Most notably your subject can't accuse you of misquoting – you will have the printed email message in your file to back you up. That can cut both ways as everyone knows that quoting verbatim doesn't always work; you may need to elide two quotes or massage the words into a different order. But the email interview gives your subject time to think, so the chances are that they will express what they really want to say more carefully. You can always email back an amended version of the quote if need be and get a quick 'agreed' in return. And then, of course, there it is digitally glidable into your article. No more need for that soul-deadening business of transcribing a tape.

Using email to interview forces you to be more prepared by formulating questions in advance. It's less intrusive, allowing you to ask your questions at any hour of the day without bothering anyone. It's also cheaper than picking up the phone every time you need to check a point.

Techniques

Online interviewing is exactly like traditional interviewing. The first email should be exploratory, introducing yourself and your publication. Use the same formality register as you would in any other circumstance; email doesn't give you a licence to be casual. Do not contact a subject by email and begin firing questions at them press-conference style, which is the online equivalent of kicking down their office door. State your intentions, and ask for permission for the interview first – then follow up with a few questions. A whole barrage of questions in one email is off-putting and will make the subject feel they are writing the article for you. It's best to bounce to and fro and build up an iterative picture. Print everything out or save it at least until after publication. Be sure to send a thank-you email and contact them again when the article comes out.

Then again, it seems that in some brands of advertorial journalism, the client is so keen to get product visibility that they're chasing the journalist. Here's one that was forwarded to me recently.

> I am looking for quotes which are opinionated, interesting, controversial and informed. Please remember to add your client's name, company, job title and the main switchboard number. Please check the deadline on Response Source and get the comments to me ASAP. Please do not send unsolicited attachments or pages of white paper or press releases. I just need good quotes I can use in the piece.
>
> Annie Gurton (freelance journalist and editor)

You might be forgiven for thinking that takes interviewing to the point of terseness, but apparently it works. We live in modern times. Response Source is an online venue set up for UK journalists to request information in a single step from over 300 organisations http://thesource.dwpub.com.

Email interviewing is a skill worth acquiring to bring your writing business into the twenty-first century, principally because it widens and enriches the range of contacts you can make. It is possible to develop meaningful email relationships – and indeed writing skills are paramount in making those relationships work. Only the written word can convey every nuance of what you want to say, so you need to think more carefully about it – where ambiguities may cause offence or lack of clarity may mean you have to keep rephrasing the question.

Email – a new art form?

Well, why not? You've read this chapter; you know all about the various ways in which the writing community uses the communication facilities of email; you've probably been emailing already and been seduced by it. Let's take it one stage further.

Just as we have had *belles lettres*, diaries and novels based on the letter form, so this new form gives rise to new ideas. There's a certain ephemerality in email that can be exciting for a writer to work with. It's forcing people to be inventive with language too – mostly in rather silly ways, unfortunately, like liberal use of emoticons and irritating intercaps, such as these:

aVANT-pOP, sUR-fICTION, hYPER-fICTION
or
ƒ ¡ (r) s † - m ø ñ d @ ¥

But we're at the beginning of many new possibilities of form. And the very fact that there are no clues at all, with the dubious exception of writing style, means two characters may not know for certain who an email partner is, and that gives rise to a new gamut of plot ploys.

Classical art has been concerned with the behaviour of form; digital art is concerned with the form of behaviour. As artists (well, I like to think that's what writers are), our task now is to invent new ways to engage with our audience. As the next chapter will show, the Net is stuffed to the gills with traditional content. What we lack are the new identities inherent in a newly structured world. There's a great deal of scope for writers to be innovative.

One might ask if computers are enabling a reinvention of the arts. Just as Art (with a capital A) is now more to do with concept and installation than with technical ability, so Writing may be veering towards performance art.

Thirty years ago the average human being communicated with 3000 people in a lifetime. That can now be achieved within a day.

Resources for Chapter 2 in Part 2 and online

3

The World Wide Web (WWW)

Network, any thing reticulated or decussated, at equal distances, with interstices between the intersections.

Dr Johnson, 1755

network, n.
[f. net n.1 + work n. Cf. Du. netwerk, G. netzwerk, Da. netværk, Sw. nätverk.]
1 e. A system of cables for the distribution of electricity to consumers; spec. one in which interconnections are such that each consumer is supplied by more than one route; hence, any system of interconnected electrical conductors or components, sometimes including a source of e.m.f., that provides more than one path for the current between any two points.

Oxford English Dictionary, 2nd edition, 1992

The World Wide Web is the nerve centre of the Internet. The writer's next stop after email.

The Web (for short) is a giant network of interconnected digital information. The term was invented by Internet pioneer Tim Berners-Lee in 1989 almost as a by-product of esoteric scientific research. But he wasn't the first to think of the concept. The theologian Pierre Teilhard de Chardin had predicted a 'noosphere' in the 1930s – a network linking mankind at the mental rather than the physical level.

It's interesting to reflect on how cross-fertilisation affects cultures. In the Industrial Revolution, the first 50 years created technologies; the second 50 years changed society because physical mobility led to a greater understanding of the rest of the world as well as a change in lifestyle in the Western world. In our information revolution, the first 50 years have created the technology and we don't yet know how the second 50 years will change society. It will almost certainly bring about an enhanced mobility of ideas. Probably it will lead to greater control over physical objects.

In Finland, which has the highest per capita concentration of mobile phones, the head of Nokia can control various functions of his house from his super-phone: he can open the front door to let visitors in while he is out on his estate; he can turn on the central heating from abroad; he can control his pot-plant watering system at a distance. All this works using computer-chip technology. One can foresee a time when every light bulb will have an IP address so that its function can be determined by more sophisticated operations than the light switch.

Science fiction writers may wonder whether micro-technology will stop at the object level. Personally, I doubt it. I can imagine a time when we will cease to rely on the Internet for all information retrieval, but will have encyclopaedias and multilingual dictionaries on programmable logic array chips physically wired to the cerebral cortex. Electro-neural interfaces are already in development and it is not beyond the bounds of possibility that before the year 2050 information will be fed directly into our brains via neural connections with machines, and the distinction between humans and machines will become blurred.

Whether we will start to wonder, at that point, if computers will have acquired consciousness, human-style, I do not know. Ada Lovelace, some 100 years ago, was already asking whether computers could acquire consciousness. No-one had an answer for her then, and I do not think anyone has the answer now.

As Niels Bohr said, 'Prediction is always difficult, especially of the future.' But of one thing we can be fairly sure – even those cortex-wired knowledge chips get their content from somewhere. The world will still have a need for writers.

Hyperlinking

But enough of all this speculation. Why talk about light bulbs having IP addresses before examining the concept of hypertext and hyperlinking. Essentially, hyperlinking is a way of jumping from a prompt word or picture to a totally different place – authoring with seven-league boots on.

Hypertext was originally conceived as a 'text space', but something rather better than text. It is named by analogy with the well-defined mathematical concept of 'hyperspace', i.e. space with more than three dimensions. (The 'hyper' in 'hypertext' means 'above': 'hyperbole' and 'hype' imply exaggeration – the first intended, the second as a result of sensational attention.)

If it's all new, imagine this. I have a set of pages on the web.

I have a biography page giving myself out as a writer, editor, speaker and craftsperson – four words underlined and in colour to indicate that something happens there. You can point the mouse arrow at any one of those four 'hats' I wear and the first screen will flip to another one. So just as my 'writer' button jumps straight to a page with my book jackets (and some sample text) and my 'craftsperson' button displays my jewellery, weaving and water-colours, so anyone else could put a link to my page into theirs.

That flip, from a link embedded in the text, is the core of hyper-linking – it is exactly like saying in a book, 'Turn to page 10,' except that the mouse click does that for you. On a grander scale, my front page can have links to New York, Santiago and Johannesburg which would also flip up following on from my own home page. That would be like saying, 'Turn to page 1,000,000.' It helps to use a book metaphor; it shows that this is a truly amazing form of publishing because anything published anywhere on the web can be linked to anything else. And it is cheap, and simple enough to be accessible to all.

What's less simple is how all this serendipitous clicking can be put to best use. Let's stick at the informational level for now and deal with the creative possibilities later on.

How to surf the web

Load up your web browser, type in an address, or click on an option on the page the browser launches into, and connect. You're surfing, browsing, navigating or researching – all amount to the same thing.

'Surf' – because when you start out you do tend to skim across the surface, clicking here and there in an aimless let's-see-what-happens way. You will get lost, waste a lot of time and find a great deal of what you come across irritating and trivial. Expect that to happen and regard it as the 'play' stage of understanding the Net – go back to being a toddler trying to fit a square block into a round hole. Allowing for playtime is an essential element in any learning process and particularly so on the Internet because its very web-like structure enables extraordinary and seemingly irrelevant juxtaposi-tions that do not occur in the course of ordinary tramline-oriented life. The playtime may mean you randomly turn up in an interest-ing place that provides inspiration. That's half the fun of it.

But having said that the best way to learn is to play, here are a few tips to catalyse your fun.

If this is your very first trip, read the section on browsers first (page 15). Then start by looking at the resource listing in Part 2, choose a place to go to and type in the address (there's no need to type out the 'http://' prefix) and press Return (Enter). Choose a short one for the first surf because later on it will be more efficient to go to this book's website and click-link from there. Then click about on the page that comes up, remembering that pictures often have links hiding behind them. There will almost certainly be an 'other links' page and before you know where you are, you will be tripping off into unexplored places, will lose complete track of where you have come from and where you are going to. That's surfing.

To convert surfing into focused research requires some dedication and a determination not to be sidetracked (see **Search engines** on page 40). It is probably worth bearing in mind that much of what you turn up will be freely available. But that's no guarantee of accuracy, accountability, reliability, completeness, frequency of update or anything else. There may come a time when you decide to turn to a commercial site (such as Lexis-Nexis or KnowUK). These offer the above guarantees as well as better quality data and judgement, improved organisation and arrangement of information and up-to-the-minute currency, and charge handsomely for it.

Web research

I've heard the web described as the lazy man's library. Physically lazy perhaps; mentally lazy, not so.

As the biggest library in the world, it receives tens of thousands of documents every day, without (as libraries do) selling off old stock. So obviously it needs sorting and classifying, and, above all, evaluating. A few years ago, that seemed like a daunting task and everyone complained about information overload and about the impossibility of finding anything on the Internet – you either got millions of hits, thousands of them irrelevant, or if there was something seemingly on the topic, there were no guarantees of its trustworthiness.

To some extent, technology will be able to do the sorting and classifying automatically. But not until people have agreed on the ways in which information should be classified, so that any part of a work can be identified and therefore retrieved. Hence the need for metadata – data about data. For example, the scale of a map and the Ordnance Survey representational icons are metadata about the map and are displayed in a key. Because we all understand the standard conventions, we can get at the information we want.

The difficulty with the Internet as a searchable repository is that we – the authoring, publishing and user communities – haven't yet agreed what the conventions in the 'key' are going to be. Some of it is familiar: take a card index catalogue in a library; the information on that card is metadata about a book. But the Internet doesn't work on a library-cataloguing model and it needs metadata about relationships between things as well. This is all quite deep stuff and not yet close to resolution. It looks as if the added value that the publisher of the future will give to a work will be the development and management of metadata. This is good news for those using the web for research. (There is a fuller section on metadata as it affects self-publishing writers in Chapter 7, pages 136-8.)

Evaluation is a human skill and that probably means that content-sorted gateways to the Internet will grow. People will be prepared to pay to circulate within a walled garden if they feel confident that the garden will contain all the best plants. Ideally, writers, researchers and journalists of all hues are looking for gateways to quality information sources for their particular discipline. Overwhelmed by the amount of information, most do not have the time or inclination to organise it all, let alone learn the intricacies of search languages. The gateway model already exists in secondary publishing (awareness services such as *Current Contents* do not list the contents of every journal, only the major ones). This model would disadvantage self-published or minority interest authors on the web, so that is why we, as writers, need to be vigilant too.

Leaving the library aspect aside, you can also use mailing lists and real-time wires, receiving tailored information and headlines on carefully chosen topics so that the content is just right for your own field of writing. You are not then tied to dialling into the Internet and can get on with writing. I get a daily bulletin from the Press Association, for example, and a weekly one from *The Bookseller*, which is as much news as I need. (Find your own news by choosing websites from the listings in Part 2, logging in to them and subscribing to any bulletins they offer.)

And heed the advice of a dedicated researcher at the cutting edge of journalism:

Panorama is the BBC's Flagship, longest running current affairs show investigating topical subjects on a range of issues. The Internet is paticularly suited to investigative journalism. The bottom line is that we have the time to invest. When we are making a programme every angle, every piece of information, every contact is spoken to initially.

The Internet and commercial databases can provide a depth and breadth that can turn a straight news piece or a hunch of an idea into an investigation. The Internet – used efficiently – can enhance the quality of the journalism. Used incorrectly it can be a huge time-waster and if sources are not double-checked, downright dangerous. The key is either training journalists or filtering the information overload for them.

Annabel Colley

A lazy man's library? Well, if you used the Internet *alone* for research, then that might be paring down to the minimum. Let me reiterate – because it's so easy to forget – the Internet is not *instead of* any other way of finding things out; it is *as well as*.

Search engines

What are they?

A search engine trawls the web for requested content. It's a glorified subject catalogue that does the footwork for you.

There's always a little box to type something in and another box saying 'Search' or 'Go' or 'Fetch' or something else. That little box actually activates the engine which hunts out words and phrases across hundreds of millions of pages of material across the entire connected world and comes back to the searcher with 'hits' – its best guesses at what you are looking for. Most engines offer 10 or 20 possibilities with a few descriptive lines so you know roughly what to expect before going to the site itself.

There's no mystique about it; just type in some well-chosen words or phrases into the box and click on 'Search' (or press Return or Enter). Then comb the results and refine the searches, and explore. It's the exploring that can lead to some interesting surprises.

If you are looking for very specific or esoteric information, you may have to try several different engines and advanced techniques. After all, no-one goes to just one library for research; they use several to discover which is the right one. Nothing's changed. There's just a tendency to blame the Internet for not being clever enough when actually it's remarkable that it's unfazed by just about any search term.

How to search

Start with a few central words and be prepared to keep trying. Writers are mostly in search of verification, interesting snippets or historical period detail. There's a difference between those requirements and a pharmaceuticals company researcher anxious to locate all references to a drug or clinical trial. The latter requires real search pros whose second tongue is Boolean logic (after George Boole, a nineteenth-century mathematician) which is touched on below.

Sophisticated searching is an art in itself and needs special training and a grasp of the difference between the many engines for maximum efficiency. Most of us will find the following tactics quite effective.

Start with a generalised, but reasonably specific search term, and type it into one of the multi-search portals listed in Part 2:3, page 167 (and on the book's website http://www.internetwriter.co.uk). My favourites are SearchIQ and AskJeeves.

SearchIQ is a good starting point because it tells you which search engine to try for your particular needs and also suggests a successful 3-phase strategy which is clearly elucidated at http://www.searchiq.com.

AskJeeves:

> only include URLs that have been evaluated by an actual living, breathing human being. So every link in the AskJeeves knowledgebase has been selected by an editor, not by some automated process.

One has to accept that the human element necessarily creates bias. This engine searches across AltaVista, Excite, Infoseek, Webcrawler and Yahoo!, which are as much as anyone would want (see below). Remember, though, that since thousands of new websites are being added each day, and thousands more are changing their URLs, the search engines are always one step behind, especially those that rely on human intervention. So vary your approaches and don't stick with the same engine all the time.

An example

If you've never used a search page before, type **http://www. askjeeves.com** into the Location/Address box of your Internet browser and press Return/Enter.

This engine uses some artificial intelligence to second-guess how you might refine the original term. So take the term 'gardens', which is clearly going to have several million hits. AskJeeves will already have excluded the gardens hobbyists on home pages and will suggest varying questions, such as:

> Where can I find helpful information and tips for <multi-choice drop-down box> gardening?
> Where can I find information on the history of gardens?
> What vegetables can I plant in June?

You can see also at a glance roughly what each engine offers and it is interesting how different they are (this applies even when the search phrase is quite specific). Top options on 'gardens' came up as follows, with a drop-down selection box of other possibilities:

AltaVista	woodworking, water gardens and fun
Excite	Desert Gardens
Infoseek	Wheelaround garden cart
Webcrawler	Royal Botanic Gardens, Kew
Yahoo!	Rama Gardens Hotel

You get about 50 possibilities instantly visible in seconds. If none applies, this is the moment to switch to whichever engine looks most likely and try again. Received wisdom is that you should not run one-word searches, but type in multiple words or a phrase in quotes to increase your chances of finding useful results. That's not necessarily true for writers who, unlike business researchers, sometimes welcome the serendipity of random inspiration.

Guessing the relevant keyword or unique combination of several words is half the battle when searching for specific information on the Internet. It always pays off to think of as many synonyms as possible and run the search several times in order to be sure of finding all material on a topic, though pinpointing exactly what to search for while trying not to spend valuable search and telephone time is quite an art.

There is a half-way house somewhere in between making a search as wide as possible and refining down so you isolate a unique phrase. Thus 'gardens' is already more specific than 'garden' which would also include 'gardening'. Typing in "18th +century +gardens" (note use of double quotes, as this is the convention) might bring up Humphrey Repton, Capability Brown, Stowe, Stourhead, Burghley House and others you had not thought of. If you just wanted Capability Brown, you would put his name in double quotes.

Search tips

Why should writers get down to deeper levels of searching? Because they may not find what they are looking for otherwise. My friend Charles Palliser, who guinea-pigged some of the historical novel research resources in Part 2 for me, wanted to find diaries. He emails:

> Looking for material relating to old diaries I found that entering the search cue "+diar* +century" in the hope of finding material on eighteenth or nineteenth century diaries elicited too much to be useful. But entering the string "century diar*" elicited sites containing the phrase "eighteenth (or nineteenth) century diaries" in small enough quantities to be useful.

The symbols are explained below. All search engines have slightly different search rules, but a few general principles can be extrapolated.

Choose useful keywords: Typing one keyword usually returns too many results to be useful. Try to narrow your search by adding refining terms. Try two related words or a phrase in double quotes (called a string) to increase your chances of finding useful results. E.g. "Alzheimer's Disease".

Use lower case. When you use lower case text, the search service finds both upper and lower case results. When you use upper case text, the search service may only find upper case. So paris will find Paris, paris and PARIS, but Paris might only launch results for Paris.

Use the asterisk as a wild card
Used at the end of a word, the asterisk (*) is like a wild card and can replace up to five characters. It allows you to broaden your search by including plurals, adjectives, adverbs and conjugated words.

So

sky*

will find pages with: sky, skylight, skywriting, skydiving, etc.

Excluding and including: The most common Boolean operators are:

AND (you're looking for all terms)
OR (you're looking for at least one of the terms)
NOT (you're excluding a term)
NEAR (you're looking for terms within a specified number of words), but this operator is not recognised by every engine.

Operators are shown in upper-case letters, although you may be able to use plus or minus signs (no spaces) to include or exclude words. Look at the instructions in the engine you are going to use regularly. They're all slightly different and the subject listings on offer, such as education, entertainment, and so on, don't succumb to complex searching at all.

Try:

(sky AND blue) AND NOT cloud (alternatively "sky +blue -cloud")

to find pages where 'sky' and 'blue' appear, but where there is no instance of the word 'cloud'.

AND and NOT may be replaced sometimes with +keyword -keyword (no spaces).

Finally, if you are a well-known writer in your field, an interesting exercise is to do a search on your own name (Excite might be a good engine and see who has been taking your name in vain. You may find your work posted up in places you didn't know about.

Which engine?

There are a lot of search engines, too many for comfort. The major ones are AltaVista, Excite, Hotbot, Infoseek, Lycos, Northern Light and Yahoo! They are listed (with several others) in Part 2:3, **Search engines** page 167. You'll just have to try your luck with them and see which one works best for your subject area. Some (Yahoo!, for example) offer a directory structure which sorts into subject categories to narrow down the search possibilities (sounds good, but doesn't work for me). The likelihood is that some of them will go out of business or be swallowed up by other companies, and I think there'll be a shake-down in the early 2000s isolating some market leaders, each with a particular specialism.

Once metadata standards are developed (described on pages 136–8) the searches will improve again. At present they return far too many suggestions, making it very difficult to cut through the irrelevant ones to find those you are actually interested in. Metadata names would facilitate search by author's name or book title or subject – any predefined field, in fact. But until web publishers have agreed to submit uniform information in a standard format we are stuck with a frustrating sense that high-quality information is out there, but the engines are not capable of finding it.

How they work

Take heart; it is destined to get better. Meanwhile, here are some things to bear in mind.

Searches all work on different principles, though all build up databases with powerful indexing and text-retrieval software. There are three components:

1. the spiders or software robots with names like 'web ferrets' or 'crawler' or 'search bots' that trawl the web looking for new pages;
2. the machine that indexes keywords (i.e. excluding prepositions, articles, parts of the verb 'to be' and so on);
3. the retrieval software that searches the index when you submit a keyword or words.

The description (or abstract) might come from the beginning of the first page of the site (something to bear in mind both when searching and when creating your own pages). They variously:

- index only the first 17 words of the page;
- search on the keywords in the current primitive meta-tagging;
- index every word;
- only index sites that have been reg
- send out software spiders that colle on the Internet.

Estimates suggest that no single search en one sixth of available web pages – and that fi in 1999 because of the increase in numbe

Northern Light indexes more pages than any of the others. The cost of maintaining ever larger databases no doubt explains why individual search engines have relatively low amounts of content indexed. Plus, it can take as much as six months for a new site to be indexed on a search engine.

So, for now, it's all a bit hit-and-miss, and the chances of missing a key site are quite high if you stick with only one engine. The ways round this are to double up the search with one of the 'parasitic' multi-search sites (listed in Part 2:3 **Multi-search portals**, page 167) which cut across five or six of the others. Or try one of the so-called personalised search agents that learn your preferences (listed in Part 2:3 **Intelligent agents**, page 168).

It's true that one of the great promises of the web is the democratising of information – making it equally available to all. I suspect we'll always have to pay for quality and that means paying for quality search facilities.

Why they're free

All search engines carry banner advertising – that's how they make their money. Most have intelligent programming of some sort so that advertisers can tie advertisements to particular search terms. AltaVista, for example, has a direct link to the Amazon bookshop and if there's a book on the subject, then you can click straight to the page describing it. Of course, Amazon also offers non-existent titles by guessing a book title to match your search terms because it has no real intelligence and is merely programmed to recognise key words.

I find I can ignore banner advertisements fairly successfully, but it's a little more insidious than that. Some engines are beginning to allow companies to pay for a 'top position' so they come up in one of the first few on the listing, and this is a trend that may grow.

Personal disk search

One of the excellent spin-offs of web engine development is that the text retrieval software is now on offer, free to any individual. ~arch all your own documents in the same way as you search the `. AltaVista Discovery is the one I use in a free downloadable ۱n http://altavista.digital.com. However, excellent and magical ‹s, I don't have it running all the time because it uses valu- ۱ory and processing resources (it indexes all your words at periodic intervals) and sits in background memory waiting to be activated. So I have it lurking in a disabled state and only load it when I really can't find any other way of winkling out a piece of buried text.

Finding a paragraph written months, or years, previously can be a frustrating experience. Computer technology only partially helps with this. In fact, it is probable that visual memory (the position on a page, the colour of the paper, etc.) is a more reliable prop than electronic text searching, or developing routines for explaining file-names that obscure the title of the piece. However, having found the bit you wanted – a date, a bibliographical reference, a quotation – it is satisfying to have it glide straight into another piece of writing.

Researchers into computers and writing divide on such competences, some saying that the disappearance of words into the maw of the computer hinders authorial confidence in their future existence; others saying that it is just a question of retraining and using new text-retrieval techniques.

The ease of retrieval and cut-and-paste has inherent dangers; it is almost always better to write something again so that it has its own integrity. Nevertheless, it is comforting to know that technology can help you find a particular formulation.

Bookmarking

Every time you come across a really useful URL, keep it. Bookmark it (in Netscape) or Add to Favorites (in Explorer) or add to Hotlist (in Opera) – browsers have different ways of referring to the same thing. It'll be somewhere on the top menu bar and the Helpfile should tell you how to do it if it isn't obvious.

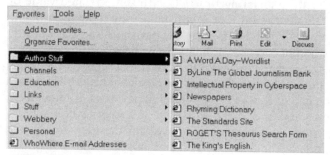

Bookmarking in Microsoft Explorer

Less easy to find is the function enabling individuals to set another page as the default. So if you do not want to dial into an advertisement bank (which is the way free ISPs set the software up) then change the location of the default page. Instructions for all three browsers are different – in Explorer it is in the Tools/Internet Options general box; in Netscape in the Options/Preferences/Appearance box; in Opera it's in the Navigation top Menu under Set Home. All hidden away, as you can see, but it is well worth digging into the program's workings to change the ISP's entry page perhaps to a favourite search engine.

If you've read the chapter up to this point without going online, now's the time to put the book down and get browsing. The next few sections in this chapter cover a few not-specially-writerly matters, but knowledge is power and it helps in using the web to best advantage.

Cookies: identifying the user

Cookies – no relation to American biscuits. They are transactional identifiers, so when you get a token on handing a coat to the cloakroom attendant, you expect to exchange it back again for your own garment at the end of the evening. That's basically a cookie. In Internet terms, cookies are bits of identification code and are both useful and also give rise to big-brother-is-watching-you anxieties. Identifiers always do. This is very roughly what happens.

Browsers will be set up to support cookies (unless changed) and that means they will accept a string of ASCII characters from a web server and store it as a 'cookie' in a file on your computer. Cookies save information about your interaction with the originating web server, typically associating its URL with some related value or identifier. That's the bit that might make one jumpy. Someone could (theoretically) find out where you have been surfing. But why would they bother for most ordinary individuals?

The upside is that cookies retain your initial registration details when you fill in a form with personal details. This is particularly useful if you had to choose a username and password. It remembers it all for you and you can get through the gateways next time. For a bookish example of cookies working well for the user, try out the 1-Click option at the Amazon UK bookshop (see Part 2:7 **Bookselling online**, pages 187-8).

And to continue the bookshop analogy, consider the way it (and other online shops) offer the ability to add items to an electronic 'basket'. As in a real shop, you put items for purchase in the basket and finally take them to the till for payment. To make this work, the server you interact with must track your movements and record your selections, since you will typically need to request several different web pages during your shopping trip. In this case, one or more cookies will be set to store the data; when you fill in your credit card details to pay, all your selections are thus passed to the server. Obviously you expect the bookshop to encrypt your user ID and password to secure it from prying eyes.

You can turn cookies off – lots of people will advise this but it's far from easy. Go to http://www.cookiecentral.com to find out how for your browser. However, it's a bit of a bore if you do as personalised settings can never be retained. This is an individual matter: turn them off if you are a paranoid sort of person; trust to Pretty Good Privacy if not.

When it all goes wrong

Error messages

One can almost always sense when a page is not going to load. It simply takes longer than usual and then pops up with the annoying error message '404 – Not Found'. Why can't they speak in plain language? Actually it is getting better. The newest versions of popular browsers take you through a context-related help screen.

If you have an older browser (version 4 or below) then remember that the Internet classes error messages which begin with a 4 (such as 400, 401, etc.) as 'Client Errors' whereas ones beginning with a 5 are 'Server Errors'.

Error 404 means that the server (the machine at the other end) is saying it's not their fault – you typed in the address wrong, or the person who put it up on the web has moved it, deleted it, or given you a slightly wrong spelling. Try a few things before giving up:

- Make sure you typed the address correctly.
- If it is a long URL with lots of directories contained in slashes, then try going back to the root (the one without slashes) and navigate from there.
- Try the Back button to find another link.

- Use a search engine to see if a new URL for the site you want comes up.

If you get a '403 – Forbidden' message then you simply don't have permission to access the document. If you get 'Server Error 500: could not fork new process', then it's their fault. Give up or try again at a less busy time (i.e. when the US is less likely to be flooding the servers).

Another annoying error is: 'unable to locate the server ... [because] the server does not have a DNS entry'. DNS stands for Domain Name Server and is basically a table. This table contains a list of names (such as 'dial.pipex.com'), and their respective numbers (such as '154.43.240.4'). Computers being computers, the machinery is actually converting the name into a number and looking for that. If it can't find an entry then it will give the above message, so check that you have entered the domain name correctly – try '.co.uk', say, instead of '.com'. It may also be that the server is temporarily unavailable, so try again later. Another possibility is that the network may be down somewhere between your computer and the server.

And then there's – 'Error 502: You have no permission to talk. Goodbye.'

Crashes

Always save the current working files before going online. If only I could remember to take that advice myself! It doesn't happen often, but machines do crash from time to time. Switch off, wait a few seconds and switch on again. No lasting harm will be done.

A crash (system freeze) may happen if you open up too many separate browser windows, give too many rapid-fire keyboard instructions, if there's a power surge, or for no obvious reason. It will *not* be a virus on a website (see **Viruses**, page 58). I have to be very careful not to move off too fast after I disconnect – the merest mouse movement sometimes immobilises the computer.

Delivery as downloading

Downloading is simply copying a set of information from one computer to another which, in Internet terms, may be countries apart.

You may be downloading web pages to the screen and keeping them in temporary memory or you may be keeping them by copying them onto your hard disk. It's like 'Save As'. You just click on the file in question and a little box should pop up to ask you where you want to put it. It is good practice to make a folder or directory on your hard disk called, say, Download with subdirectories running off it which you can sort files into later. The first time you download a file from the Internet, you will be asked where you want it saved to (e.g. /Download); after that the software should remember that as the last location in which you placed a downloaded file and will offer it again next time. It is easy to swap between your various Download subdirectories.

If no box pops up, then the file could be going into a temporary directory, so if it apparently disappears from view, see if you can find it either in a folder labelled/Temp (PC) or Desktop Folder (Mac).

It's comforting when the progress of the download is shown in a pop-up box telling you how many minutes it is going to take (invariably a miscalculation, incidentally). If that does not happen, the progress bar of the browser in the lower right corner shows by the length of the moving blue bar how much longer it is going to take.

When downloading a suite of web pages, or a piece of software or a very long document then it will probably be compressed so that it is quicker to transmit. The extension letters SEA, HQX or SIT (for the Mac) and ZIP (for the PC) are the give-away signs. You will not be able to read the material until you have unpacked it. If double-clicking on the file name yields no results, then you will have to download a piece of shareware software to do it for you (see Part 2:1 **Web access tools**, page 161).

I should mention that you can also download files by FTP which stands for File Transfer Protocol – the same sort of stable as TCP/IP. But quite frankly it is so much easier just to stick with web pages that I wouldn't bother unless there is a compelling reason.

Publishing as uploading

Uploading is basically synonymous with Internet publishing (as far as writers are concerned) and I suspect the two words will soon be interchangeable.

Uploading is also done by FTP, which has become a word now with a verbal form that no-one is sure how to spell, as in: 'I have ftp'd the document up to my home page.' Again, you need some dedicated software so if it isn't provided as part of your joining package, then see Part 2:1 **Web access tools**, page 161. (More detail on self-publishing is in Chapter 7.)

Although FTP is very simple, it may be puzzling at first because your Internet Service Provider may not have used plain English to tell you exactly how to set it up so you can get at the web space on offer. (Your area is password-protected – so that only authorised people can alter material on the site.) Get some technical support the first time even if you have to pay for it. After that, the software will remember the settings (save them first) and after that ftp-ing will be easier than posting a parcel – much easier.

Cluttering the hard disk: storage and caching

All this downloading and uploading requires storage space. The more disk space you have the more versatile your use of the Internet can be. The machine will keep web pages in temporary memory for a chosen number of days. That means you can go online, load several pages and then go off-line and read them at leisure. If you have enough space allocated, then it can re-present most of these pages again three weeks later without dialling in to the Internet again. This is called 'caching'.

Cached files sit in a directory called Temporary Internet Files (on the PC) or the Cache folder (on the Mac), usually located in the browser's preferences folder. If you have enough disk space, you should allocate about 250 Mb to it (in the Internet Settings). Don't do this unless you have a fast machine because the downside is that allocating a lot of space here may slow down the efficiency of your computer.

Storage capacity allows your own machine to become a filing cabinet. It is useful to save textual information found on a website because you may not come across it again. Some people prefer to print out and file paper in physical files, but I like to keep the electronic versions with sensible names of my own as I then know where to find them – and they also succumb to text-retrieval searches (see **Search engines**, page 40). Of course, saving or printing are both forms of copying and are subject to the same legal restrictions as any other form of copying. Generally speaking, this falls into the category of time-shifting – like video-ing a television film to view at a convenient time – and the assumption is that people will delete copyright materials when they've had time to look at them. Don't forget that anyone's web pages are in copyright whether they have a copyright notice on them or not. Those that do will more often than not carry a line like this:

> This publication may be freely copied and/or distributed in its entirety. However, individual sections MAY NOT be copied and/or distributed without the prior written agreement of the publishers.

If you have an older machine (say pre-1998) then you may not have a hard disk larger than 1 Gb, and though that sounds like plenty, it may not offer the luxury of unbounded electronic storage. Think about getting a writable CD drive, a second hard disk or a zip drive – in that order.

You'll be surprised how much disk space email messages take up – assuming you keep them all filed for future reference. This is particularly so if people send you attachments with pictures or sound and video clips – and even writers will find themselves rapidly getting involved with the other media. Bear in mind that:

> 1 Mb = 250 pp text = 1 page-sized still image = 5 seconds of sound = 0.3 seconds of moving pictures.

Roughly speaking, one character occupies one byte and there are, on average, six bytes to a word. So 64K is equivalent to about 10,000 words.

Plug-ins: the extra bits

Sometimes you will arrive at a site and a message will pop up to say that you can't view it properly because there's another bit of software you need to attach – or plug in – to your browser. Hence the expression 'plug-in'. It's a bit like having different lenses for your camera: wide-angle, close-up and so on. So on a browser, the plug-ins are there to allow the user access to music, or broadcast-quality sound, or video, animation effects or protected documents.

The site in question should automatically link to the source of the plug-in and, subject to your clicking a 'yes' button, the whole thing will happen all by itself because most of them are free. The only trouble is that there are no standards and sound or video clips come in lots of different formats, all needing their own plug-in. The only cause for anxiety would be a vague unease about littering your hard disk with too much software. And you'd be right, up to a point. Lean-and-mean is a good maxim for computer efficiency. On the PC, some of these plug-ins insist on pre-loading a short-cut into memory in case they're needed. This slightly slows up the efficiency of the computer, though you can disable them from the Start menu. The Apple menu and Launcher work in a different manner anyway. But plug-in-o-mania is the price you pay for the full razzle-dazzle of the Internet.

These are the plug-ins writers would benefit from, either as users or when you come to create your own web pages (see Chapter 7). Sources of all these are listed in Part 2:1 **Web access tools**, page 161.

Document exchange – the Acrobat Reader

This is an add-on every writer needs because (as Chapter 1 says) published documents are often put on the Net in PDF format to preserve all formatting. This is known as 'locked', meaning that the user can only read the text and cannot alter it. There should be a link on web pages to the free Acrobat Reader http://www. adobe.com/products/acrobat/readstep.html. Less obvious is how to tweak the browser settings to choose between automatically launching a PDF file into the Acrobat Reader or saving it to disk. The default will be an automatic launch and that's fine for those who intend to print out. But if you are happy reading on-screen and want to save to read later, then get some help – it's in the settings in Netscape and Opera, and with a right mouse-click in Explorer.

Typically software like this will offer the Reader free, and charge for the full-blown product – the logic is obvious: the producers need to generate a market. To create files in this format you will need to buy Acrobat Exchange. As a reader, you won't need it, but to publish or deliver longer texts on the web, you will.

PDF is a format based on page-description-language technology, so however you make a PDF document, you are in a sense 'printing' it – either directly to a PDF representation, or to an intermediate PostScript representation which is subsequently converted to PDF.

In theory, files can be shared, viewed, navigated and printed exactly as intended by anyone with a free Adobe Acrobat Reader though there can be a slight problem because of the different standard paper sizes used in the UK and the US. It depends whether the publication is in portrait or landscape, but either way if it's laid out for the slightly larger size then one or two lines might spill over onto another page. It's best to design your document to fit within the width of A4 and the height of US Letter. This means that you make a custom page size for your document of 279 mm deep by 210 mm wide.

When such a document is printed to make a PDF file, the printer-driver options will expect a sheet size such as A4 to which your document page, albeit smaller, is printed. As a result, when the PDF is opened in Acrobat, it will be set to A4 or US Letter size. The solution here (my friend Conrad Taylor tells me) is to use Acrobat Exchange (in version 4, confusingly now just known as 'Acrobat') to crop all of the pages down to 279 x 210 mm, and re-save the file.

There is a 'fix' at the Reader end too which you may need for incoming documents originating in the US – the print dialogue has an option 'shrink to fit'; select that, and Acrobat should scale each page to fit onto the currently selected paper size.

For those who use Word (as many writers do) it is a mistake to assume that a Word document converts identically to a PDF file with line-for-line accuracy. This is because Word's printing technology has a weakness in this area. Self-publishers should use a dedicated desk-top publishing package when distilling files for PDF usage.

Sound on the Net – RealAudio, LiquidAudio

For audio, the standard technology is MP3 (MPEG-1 Audio Layer-3) which is a format for compressing a sound sequence into a very small, high quality file.

The RealPlayer (and RealProducer) both come in a free version. Producer allows you to create sound and video clips to put on a website; the RealPlayer lets you hear them. This is one of the ones that insinuates itself into the start-up routine because it is so confident you will want to use it all the time. As indeed one might, because RealAudio and RealVideo capabilities give tune-in access to radio and TV stations by the thousand, though until telephone metering ceases to clock up the pennies in the UK, most sensible people would give them a miss. Make sure you have a newish and fairly powerful computer with all the right sound and video cards and lots of memory.

At a simpler level, RealPlayer enables you to hear poetry and talking books being read from a website (copyright-cleared, one hopes). The technology is here – the economic logic is somewhat fuzzy.

By contrast, LiquidAudio has been working with the music industry to supply copyright-cleared tracks from CDs so it both delivers sound and acts as a rights management system. Liquid-Audio 'gives artists and labels the software and services to distribute their music online, while protecting their rights at every step'. This is an interesting development which should rub off on writers too. The (free) Liquid Music Player also displays lyrics, information about the artists and stills from promotional videos.

Moving images – QuickTime

This is for displaying (and editing) moving pictures. QuickTime used to be a bit of a nightmare in the CD-ROM era because you never knew whether you had the latest version of it and every CD seemed to want to dump yet another version on your hard disk. This is now largely solved and QuickTime is to be adopted as a standard by the Moving Picture Expert Group (MPEG). Those interested in story-telling through animations will need QuickTime.

Animations – Shockwave and Flash

These are both free from Macromedia which specialises in animations and interactive elements. Flash is good for movie clips, advertisements and webTV; Shockwave lets you view interactive web content like games, business presentations and various entertainment sites. Both are designer tools and more or less essential to any multimedia project.

These main web file types you will come across are on the opposite page.

Format	Brief definition	Use for writers
ASCII (American Standard Code for Information Interchange)	Plain text files	Email Exchanging files in incompatible word processors
GIF (Graphics Interchange Format)	Standard format for compressing images on the web	Buttons and pictures on your web pages
HTML (HyperText Markup Language) or XML (eXtensible Markup Language)	Standard format for displaying pages on the web	Basis of web pages: writers need to know about it but it's not essential to know how to write it
JPEG (Joint Photographic Experts Group)	Standard format for compressing images on the web (more complex pictures than GIFs)	You'd use JPEGs (pronounced jaypeg) for your photograph: people like to see who they are talking to
MPEG (Moving Picture Experts Group)	Standard for compressing digital video and audio	MP3 is a standard for this: of interest to broadcasters and for music downloading
PDF (Portable Document Format)	Format for presenting printed documents electronically so that they appear exactly as they would on a printed page	Good for Internet publishing because of its compression and security features
RealAudio/ LiquidAudio	Means of playing an audio file as it is downloading, rather than having to download and store it first	Of interest to writers for broadcasting
RealVideo	Means of playing a video file as it is downloading, rather than having to download and store it first	Of interest to writers for film, TV and broadcasting

Advertising

One of the most extraordinary aspects of the Internet is the 'free' ethic that prevails. This is cosy when you are the consumer, and annoying when you are the provider.

Free services come at a price – free ISPs carry advertising to pay for them. Some firms are even giving away computers to those willing to give lots of details about themselves so that they can be bombarded with specially targeted advertising

The projected figure for the number of people online in the year 2000 is 237 million – the breakdown being roughly half English speaking and slightly over half non-English. You can update that figure as the year progresses at http://www.nua.ie/surveys/how_many_online.

That represents a significant advertising market and banner

adverts are going to become more frequent, possibly more obtrusive and maybe more personally tailored. Web robots will learn an individual's buying patterns and present advertising materials that are likely to appeal on the basis of what the user has bought before. This strikes some as a bit Big Brother-ish – why shouldn't you have the freedom to be serendipitous in your tastes and how dare someone predict what you might buy!

Most of my writing colleagues resent advertising coming into their own homes and on to their PC screens with a vehemence normally reserved for door-to-door ironing-board-cover salesmen. They should bear in mind that they're quite easy to ignore and banner advertising is, after all, paying for all the freely available information we have come to expect from the Internet. The advantages to advertisers go something like this:

- Advertisers can underwrite content and give readers who view advertisements free access to it. They can sponsor competitions so that readers who click on advertisements could win full subscriptions to a publication.
- Readers can be offered a choice between having advertisements along with content, at a lower subscription cost, or having advertising-free content at a higher subscription cost.
- An advertiser can gain valuable insights into a targeted audience by using special product discount coupons and promotions that elicit feedback on basic information such as buying habits, hobbies, household size, location and family size. You might say that advertising on the Internet is akin to free market research.

Remember also that in the nineteenth and early twentieth centuries books commonly carried advertising and some still do in a disguised form – lists of books in the same series or by the same author. I think we may have to get used to the idea that advertising will seep into online life just as it has on commercial television. Who knows, it may even become a new art form.

Viruses: assessing the threat

You are not more likely to pick up a virus on the Internet than by any other means. Most shareware sites and home pages of companies offering trial or freeware are extremely careful about virus protection. They cannot afford not to be.

Everyone, however, gets warnings from well-meaning friends saying that if you get an email with the title 'such and such' you should not open it because it contains a virus that will destroy all your work. More often than not, this is a hoax. Some sort of pleasure evidently pertains to the promulgating of hoaxes. Do not worry – you will not get a virus just by reading the message. You may get one by opening up an attachment file (page 23). You'll see a little paperclip symbol bullet-pointing the incoming message. If in doubt just delete the whole message without opening the attachment. To be really safe, don't open attachments from any unrecognised source.

Viruses are invisible programs capable of replicating themselves and ruining work. Some are malignant, some benign. At best they can be annoying, but are curable; at worst they can corrupt an entire hard disk. The good news for writers is that they are uncommon in text files as they are normally attached to program codes – so day-to-day document exchange between colleagues is very unlikely to be a worry.

Still, the time to worry about viruses is *before* your computer gets one. Get a virus detector which activates every time you switch on your computer. It will automatically scan the contents of the hard disk and check for the 10,000-odd known viruses. When you try to open an infected file, the virus detector program activates and a box will pop up to tell you if it has a virus. You *must* have the most up-to-date version to be secure because new viruses appear all the time.

How do you know you have got a virus? You will recognise a virus if a familiar application starts behaving in an unfamiliar way, or the screen display inexplicably produces a strange phenomenon – characters falling to the bottom of the display, printing of rectangular blocks on the screen, system crashes, and reformatting of the hard disk are among the possible delights.

If you do discover you have a virus, stay calm and follow the instructions in the disinfecting software *to the letter* even if you do not understand a word of it. And remember to backup, backup and backup your work before anything awful happens to it.

The perpetrators of hoaxes and viruses are not necessarily vandals (even though the effects are comparable to house-breaking). Some regard virus-spreading as a morally justifiable act. The world, they say, is getting too dependent on computers, both in businesses and in governments. One way of counteracting monopolies and political control is to destroy that dependence. You can agree with that or not, as you will. I am not sure that politics came into it the time I wasted a whole day getting rid of a virus. Updates are in Part 2:3 **Viruses and hoaxes**.

Resources for Chapter 3 in Part 2 and online

4.

Virtual communities

HANA: This is a very important office memorandum, Mr Gross.
GROSS: It looks like a hodge-podge of entirely haphazard groups of letters.
HANA: Perhaps, at first glance. But there's method in it. It's in Ptydepe, you
see... A new office language which is being introduced into our organisation.

Vaclav Havel, *The Memorandum*

We have looked at the Internet versions of letter-writing and
research. This chapter is about joining clubs. Virtual communities
are associations of people who 'meet' online. Some are membership societies, while others are open to all. They are built around
three main elements:

- a website;
- a discussion area for members (an email list or a web-based
  real-time interaction). These are variously called
  newsgroups, forums, listservs [sic] or chat rooms;
- an emailed newsletter (also called an e-zine or web-zine).

Items 2 and 3 above overlap. The current information arrives in
your mailbox; the archive of previous topics is posted on a website.
Messages are called 'postings' and they are very informal, of variable quality and tend to be of the 'someone has a query or a comment: someone else answers it' variety.

Discussion areas fall into these classes:

- Unmoderated: anyone can subscribe and everyone on the list
  receives every email.
- Moderated: anyone can subscribe and the list-owner can
  throw people off who 'flame' (get rude, irritating or talk too
  much) and also monitors the postings before they go out to
  the list.
- Closed mailing lists: only the moderator can email out to the
  group and consolidates all the points of interest so that you
  get a magazine-type mailing.

Forums: unmoderated and moderated

There are thousands of newsgroups on a network linked to the Internet called Usenet. Every special interest, hobby or professional grouping is represented here – food-and-drink buffs, violin-makers, model-aeroplane hobbyists, meteorologists, fast-car freaks, depressives, diabetics, pagans, cinema-lovers – everything. That causes concern because the laws of freedom of speech mean that many groups go uncensored. The individual, however, can get filtering software to exclude undesirables – so, if there are children in the house, access can be restricted (NetNanny is one brand name and there are others).

Unmoderated newsgroups suffer from an overdose of dross, and the writing ones are no exception. It is worth breezing in and out of a few, just to see what they offer, but you'll probably find them full of creative-writing aspirants operating at a very naive level. You'll have to go through the laborious process of downloading a list of newsgroups when you first log on to the news server (instructions for doing this vary from one ISP to another) or here's a starter handful – and I'm not saying I recommend any of these:

> misc.writing
> misc.writing.screenplays
> ucd.rec.poetry
> alt.poetry.doggerel
> rec.arts.books.hist-fiction
> alt.usage.english

Newsgroups are a bit like the Letters to the Editor pages of newspapers. And, in similar fashion, some names seem to dominate – just as they do in the *London Review of Books*. It's not such a different world.

FAQs

The FAQ or compilation of Frequently Asked Questions originated in the newsgroup environment and has since become a feature of web pages too. The idea is that people should take some responsibility for finding out how to operate the particular system themselves before bothering others needlessly. You may have a query that has already been answered. Obviously it wastes less time if you trawl the FAQ first. People tend to forget this and perhaps with good reason: the writers of FAQs are often computer technicians who have no real understanding of how people look for information and how to make it easy for them to find it. If you are interested in a particular subject area, it is worth being a little patient.

Here's the beginning of extensive welcoming material in a newsgroup mentioned above which comes from a literate FAQ:

> alt.usage.english is a newsgroup where we discuss the English language. We discuss how particular words, phrases, and syntactic forms are used; how they originated; and where in the English-speaking world they're prevalent. (All this is called "description".) We also discuss how we think they *should* be used ("prescription").
>
> alt.usage.english is for everyone, *not* only for linguists, native speakers, or descriptivists.
>
> Guidelines for posting
>
> ───────────────
>
> Things you may want to consider avoiding when posting here:
>
> (1) re-opening topics (such as singular "they" and "hopefully") that experience has shown lead to circular debate.
> (2) questions that can be answered by simple reference to a dictionary.

On the whole, the good groups tend to organise their material and put it on a website in a more useful format than the uninhibited, and undisciplined, splurge of the average newsgroup. Misc.writing postings, for example, are archived on a website, as are some other lists (see Part 2:4 **Critiquing and writing workshops**, page 169 and Part 2:3 **Education and teaching writing**, page 163).

Specialist subjects

That said, newsgroups can be useful for novel writers researching characters. You can subscribe to a group and just read the notes people have posted up (that is called lurking), or you can post one up yourself if you need a detail that you think someone could answer. I was at one time writing a novel with a wine buff as its hero and I joined rec.food.drink and asked questions. People were astonishingly helpful, shared information and offered me ideas for my character that I simply would never have thought of. This sort of response was typical:

Wow - you novelists! - what you won't do for the sake of veracity! :)
But seriously, I'd be happy to communicate with you on this subject.

Or you can join a discussion group – or thread, as it is called. Many
are extremely lively and you can quite easily find yourself making
new, remote friends. In fact, it is known to be addictive. I came
across someone the other day who subscribes to 256 newsgroups
and so spends 8–10 hours a day dealing with her correspondence.
Internet Addiction Disorder has become a serious modern malady.

Writers' circles

When I was a columnist for *Writers' News*, a reader who lived in
Israel wrote to me. Did I know of any British Writers' Circles
online, he asked, because he would like to join one. And if he
wanted to, then was it not likely that other readers did too? At that
time, there was no group based in the UK – at any rate not one
open to all-comers. So he joined one called WRITE, which originated in the US. 'Frankly,' he emailed, 'I have come round to seeing that the New/Old World divide really doesn't matter that
much.' Since participants are reading and critiquing each other's
work, that sounds like fair comment.

Below are four groups that seem established enough not to disappear over the turn of the millennium and I am giving details of
them so that you can see the kind of thing you might expect before
plunging in to the resource listing in Part 2:4, page 169 where
you'll find links to other groups. My advice would be to look at the
websites first and only subscribe if you really want to. On some
sites it can appear as if the blind are leading the blind. The details
of how to join an email circle will be on the site.

WRITE and REWRITE

http://www.writelinks.com

There are three closed lists on this site and you have to fill in an
application form online. These are much smaller groups – inten-
tionally limited in size so that it generates maybe 8–10 messages
a day – much easier to handle, but still a commitment. This is a
serious and sensitive venue which has a moderator who screens out

anything she considers unsuitable. Janet Kent formed WRITE when she was looking for a place to share her own creative efforts and to receive some feedback on her work. She could not find anything suitable, so she decided to start her own group and it has snowballed from there.

There are no 'lurkers' here in order to protect the efforts of members. In fact, though it was free in its earlier inception, it now makes a charge of $5 a month to cover administration and (perhaps) to ensure that those who join are seriously committed to making it work. The purpose of the group is to give writers a place for sharing work-in-progress with other writers and for receiving constructive feedback to help them polish and improve that work. Only members can post or receive mail and the moderators ensure that members are all serious writers. There is no genre sorting, and both published and still-to-be published authors share views on fiction and non-fiction, poetry and prose. It is a working group and not a place for social chatter or anything that does not relate directly to the craft of writing.

The site also notes: 'There is a major distinction between helpful comments from professionals and well-meaning but useless or possibly harmful comments from other people who may read the manuscript.' So it also offers professional evaluations of work by a person who, 'through experience and knowledge of the marketplace, has acquired expertise to judge it objectively.' I haven't sampled this service, but there is much sensible advice on the site and it is worth visiting.

The Writing Workshop

email to: writing-request@lists.psu.edu
http://www.geocities.com/~lkraus/workshop/index.html

There used to be four sublists in this circle, now there are ten: Fiction, Non-fiction, Poetry, Novels, Script-writing, Young Adult Writing (YAWrite), Prose-Poetry and Flash Fiction (Prose-P), and Romance writing (LoveStory-L) and Teen for the under 18s.

Automatic subscription is not allowed for these lists; instead the request is passed on to the list owner who provides the applicant with further information on the list and on how to join. There are also some workshop rules: that you have to be serious about writing, that you don't show anything circulated to the list to anyone else, and that you must participate in the workshop by submitting and commenting on work about every two weeks.

There are three subscription options for the lists:

MAIL – you get every message posted to the list immediately.

DIGEST – you receive a digest version of the list once or twice a day, containing the text of all messages since the last digest. (Digests may be up to 70K in size so that indicates the extent of the traffic.)

NOMAIL – suppresses sending of list mail when you need a break.

Online Writing Community

email to: mailbase@mailbase.ac.uk
message: join trace <your.name>
http://trace.ntu.ac.uk

This one originates from an English university, but is as international as the others. It is a 24-hour community for writers and readers across the world with a particular emphasis on online interactions, so although you can just join the list, the real activity spurs off the website. Participants write, critique each other's work, discuss books and chat online.

Conferences are generally moderated with groups on writing and children; reading matters; writers and society; and an unmoderated writing workshop. There is also a writer-in-residence, competitions and the opportunity to contribute to interactive fiction or to discussion points such as this one:

OPINION: trAce will feature personal views of the Internet by writers at the forefront of the debate. Every month there will be a new article and a chance for you to respond and join the discussion.

Kicking off is Australian author Dale Spender, who believes everyone should be given a computer free of charge. She says:

"The raw material of today's global community is intellectuality and creativity, which is why everyone needs a computer, an ISP, a national information infrastructure, and a support system. The government who buys every member of society a computer is sure to get a great deal, and excellent customer service agreement. Not to mention a head start in the global economy."

Do you agree?

The Hitchhiker's Guide To The Galaxy

http://www.h2g2.com

This is a little hard to place; it is not a forum exactly, nor a writers' circle, nor a chat room, nor a fan-club, but it has elements of all four and it is certainly a community. It's what I called above multi-authored patchwork. This is a quirky site that opened while I was writing this book and it is worth including because Douglas Adams, the author of the above-titled book, was one of the first two British writers to have a fan-club on the Usenet newsgroups (the other was Terry Pratchett and I remember that because I was doing some research on fan-clubs at the time).

This site aims to make Adams' original vision of a Guide to the Galaxy come true. The idea was that it would offer advice about almost any place, object, entity or event anyone could think of. It would be a handheld device, able to tap into vast resources of information, culture and life. To make that dream come true (and I believe it did start as a dream), the site is gathering knowledge and opinion which will one day be accessible through the imagined device which the site is calling h2g2. It bills itself as consisting of hundreds of entries on subjects ranging from *aerosol deodorants* to *zoos*. These are not like encyclopaedia entries. To give you a flavour, take this one on writers.

> Writers
> They don't like talking.
>
> Strange and mysterious creatures who work alone in darkened spaces. When encouraged by kind words, a writer can be openly gregarious to the point of excess. They are mostly incredibly witty, and underneath the layers of unwashed, unkempt creativity, are usually beautiful souls to spend time with.
>
> Alternatively, they are also known as people who enjoy only their own company, deliberately keep antisocial hours to avoid contact with others, and delight in torturing themselves in order that they might finally have something to write about. Writers, in an odd shift of physical precedent, rarely ever get what's coming to them.
>
> The Hitchhiker's Guide To The Galaxy
> *Editor ID*: A2214

There follow several postings, e.g.

Is it safe to allow writers to form groups? Should we keep them segregated or allow them to mingle freely with other people in darkened rooms?

And

As long as we can make money out of it. Hey – I just had a thought, does contributing to this website mean I'm a writer? Argh! Help!

This form of collaborative patchwork is growing – where 'interactive' means that users help to create and reshape the work itself.

Newsletters

Closed lists are sent out as emailed newsletters – daily, weekly, monthly, as the moderator (a type of editor) chooses. They do not arrive haphazardly, like topic discussions in newsgroups, so you know what you are letting yourself in for when you subscribe.

There are many excellent newsletters and you will have to follow your own interests to find them. See Part 2:4 **Newsletters**, page 168 as well as the genre listings in Part 2:6, pages 174–86 for some suggestions. Visit the website first and then follow the joining instructions.

One that deserves a special mention is Free Pint – a free email newsletter offering tips, tricks and articles on how and where to find reliable information on the Internet. It is written by information professionals in the UK and is sent to more than 20,000 subscribers every two weeks. It is useful for writers in a wide range of non-fiction disciplines. Look at it on **http://www.freepint.co.uk**.

There are a number of different ways of generating such mailing lists; the better ones have a two-tier registration so that the person joining has to authenticate their subscription. It's always free, so it isn't a subscription in the usual meaning of the word, but because the volume of traffic can be high you'll want to decide for yourself whether to have mailbox overflow.

I foresee a growing trend here as standards improve and quality control becomes the norm. High-flying specialist business information sheets – which currently command exorbitant prices because of their specialist targeted knowledge – may start to be circulated by email once security is established.

Mailing lists offer some new opportunities for writers because they are developing into e-zines. I've not yet come across any of these that pay contributors, but times may change.

Mailing lists

Mailings lists are hosted by a 'list server', which is a computer equipped with a piece of list-management software. Majordomo, listserv [sic] and mailbase are the best known, though mailbase is only available to the academic community. The other two are available to anyone who wants to start a list, but they are far from easy to set up and require a knowledge of scripting and compiling. There are other, easier, sources if you want to set up a list on your own site. See Part 2:4 **Mailing lists**, page 170.

Internet Chat

Internet Relay Chat (IRC) is a way of talking – via your keyboard – in real time with people all over the world. Sound and video chat is just a step away. It is an eerie experience. The computer, logged on to the Internet, transmits your typing directly to someone else's screen. This is synchronous communication that is not quite like spoken or written language yet uses conventions from both. It is a written form that is transmitted, received and responded to within a time frame that has formerly been only thought relevant to spoken communication.

This is the world of 'muds' and 'moos', silly words that describe a conferencing system that can be a life-line for writers working in remote parts or for genre writers sharing a specialised interest. Writing groups arrange to 'meet' online at a specified time.

Some real chat

To give you some idea about how it operates, here is the beginning of a Moo. You can see from this that the medium is adaptable to serious conferencing:

[The Moo begins here. Several formal sections are omitted; others shortened]

Sue says, "Hello everyone and welcome to the trAce meeting room at LinguaMOO."

Sue says, "Sometimes online meetings are held to discuss work which has already been posted to the web, but others are like this one. In this case, the formal sections of my talk have been prepared beforehand

and I will paste them to the screen in small paragraphs as if I were speaking to you direct."

Carolyn arrives.

Rogerg arrives from Tutorial.

Sue says, "trAce is funded by the Arts Council of England but we have members in 18 countries around the world. Our principal language is English although for many of our members that is their second or third tongue. Although we claim to use the 'English' language in cyberspace, this does not necessarily mean that we actually understand each other."

Jan lost his connection and had to reconnect.

Jan sits down quietly and listens to Sue.

Jan nods at Sue.

Carolyn smiles at Sue.

Sue says, "It's important we use the Internet not just to strengthen our own local identities, but also to nourish and develop a sense of collaborative global culture. Does anyone have any points they'd like to raise from what I have said so far?"

Carolyn grins.

debbiegaunt arrives.

olaf says, "I guess I smile too"

Sue says, "carolyn asks how we overcome the language differences"

Relationships are often begun in chat rooms and are creatively continued by email afterwards. It can simply be an extension of the time-honoured tradition of writers meeting in a literary pub.

You just have to find the right 'pub'. I am sorry to say that if you experiment with one of the chat rooms attached to a search engine such as Yahoo! and others, you will be astonished at the quantities of complete idle nonsense.

There are all sorts of issues about whether people are who they really say they are or masquerading for the purposes of a personal or experimental fiction as someone of another sex, background or age. Unless people are careful and make their own rules for their own chat groups, this form of communication spirals very quickly into the realms of fantasy and unreality. Some people love that. I have tried to get involved and I have well-respected novelist friends who are addicted to it. But that, I think, is the point. You either get passionate, and I'm prepared to take on trust that the experience is interesting and the rewards unusual, or you decide to leave it alone.

One view is that creative writers dealing with issues of pain and emotionally charged experience may often find validation of their own interpretations by interacting with other people who are also trying to articulate ideas and dramas of universal significance. I understand from fellow writers that chat rooms can enable an imaginative flow by providing confidence-building back-up.

I feel bound to come clean here and confess that I find Chat has a trivialising quality that makes serious interchange awkward; not impossible, but yet further removed from the personal. Everyone is reduced to the common denominator of speech-in-print, with no visual or verbal clues; despite the loose existence of rules of behaviour and chat protocol, it's distressingly anarchic. Aimless chat is the insidious seduction of the Internet; it can replace inward contemplation and real experience, thereby driving out the motive impulse that a writer needs in order to *write*.

Internet conferencing

Chat may come into its own when supplemented with video-conferencing. The software available at present is a poor substitute for real face-to-face experience. But it will – eventually – bring non-verbal communication, body language and various inter-personal cues onto the Internet along with the text, sound and graphics capacities we have already. There are many unexplored performance art and filmic possibilities here.

Unfortunately it requires expensive dedicated software and a video camera that sits on top of the monitor at each participating machine. It only works with a speedy ISDN line or better. Direct dial-up video-conference sessions can only go between participating machines with compatible conferencing software.

Video-conferencing offers two-way interactive video with audio and graphics exchange. So people can talk to each other in real time, share and discuss documents or drawings, and see each other (the camera can rotate to focus on different people).

Picture quality is very poor (about one fifth of television resolution and very grainy and jumpy) and lack of sufficient bandwidth is a problem that remains to be solved, but it will be. Not only will writers then be able to communicate almost as if they were sitting side by side over the manuscript, but grandparents will be able to relate to grandchildren across the globe. Watch developments.

Writer's block

What, I hear you ask, is the subject of writer's block doing in the virtual communities section of a guide to the Internet? In truth, the proper place for it might well be the therapist's couch. But since that is not always an option, is there anything that technology can supply when you are faced with that appalling patch of white-space phobia, when the words just won't flow and all your creativity seems to have dried up? Oddly enough, this lonely activity gives rise to so much community interest that it seemed worth examining what help you can get online.

First, not everyone is convinced that writer's block hits technophobes and technophiles alike. Many claim that the word-processor has driven writer's block out. The reason for this may well be the temporary nature of a first written draft: it is so easy to rewrite that the fear of the blank page or screen is less threatening.

Help online

Yet, if technology has hit at writer's block, how curious it is that many sites devoted to it have sprung up on the web. These all seem to be well-visited, yet every caller is necessarily a word-processor user.

If you suffer a lot, it could be worth browsing at random through other writers' hints on what works to get themselves 'unstuck'. You'll find a selection from the sensible to the zany in Part 2:4 **Critiquing and writing workshops**, page 169. My own personal technique, which has nothing to do with technology, is to stop writing for the day in the middle of a sentence. Next day you will be forced to finish it before continuing.

Writer's block is a dis-ease that people do not always own up to, but it hits even the most experienced writer from time to time. T S Eliot had writer's block most of his life. Sometimes, there really is something fundamentally wrong with the motive idea. Or perhaps it is just a case of realising that you have to cave in and switch the computer off for the rest of the day or week. But for those who are paralysed for weeks or months it is a lonely business. In such circumstances you may feel you are hitting your head against a brick wall. It is worth trying anything. Even whatever Internet technology has to offer.

Resources for Chapter 4 in Part 2 and online

5.

Electronic imprints

So, Reader, having now discharg'd my Conscience of a small Discovery
which I thought my self obliged to make to thee, I proceed to tell thee, that
our Friend Aurelian had by this time danced himself into a Net which he
neither could, nor which is worse desired to untangle.

William Congreve, *Incognita*, 1692

An electronic imprint is digitised content designed to be read on a
computer screen, or on a dedicated hand-held machine. It can be
bought direct from a website or from a traditional bookshop.

Isaac Asimov once wrote an essay in which he described the
ideal medium for information. It should, he thought, be optimally
ordered, the medium should have a low energy requirement and
should be portable. The acronym for that comes from Bound Optimally Ordered Knowledge – BOOK.

Most of us will have a mental picture denoting 'book' ranging
from vellum-bound to gold-tooled calfskin to yellow-edged paperback. Should we be adding plastic-boxed, battery-operated screen
to that image?

It is hard to endow such a visualisation with the same aesthetic
pleasure as a crimson buckram slipcase, the feathering of marbled
endpapers or the gilt of a laminated letter. We are entering an 'e'
lingua – where 'electronic' gets cut down to size in a selection of
'e'-words that do not trip easily off the tongue. There's the
e-book, e-zine, e-journal and e-newspaper (the content); the
e-reader (the hardware); and the e-ink and e-paper that carry the
imprints. And just to get all the cringing over in one go, some
people are calling paper-based editions 'p-books'.

The debate on whether traditional books are dying out continues. The general feeling appears to be that they are not – online
publications are *as well as* not *instead of*. We should keep the new
technology in proportion, avoiding the emphasis that is being put
on the techniques for assembling and transmitting the message at
the expense of the content of the message and the way it is ordered.

The Internet doesn't change the criteria by which society judges good writing; it just makes more of it available and in different forms. It is, at its simplest level, only a delivery mechanism.

Internet-only imprints

Internet-only imprints are only available on websites. At the planning stage of this book, I imagined this would be a long section, bursting with ideas for as yet unpublished authors to find venues for marketing their work. I'm afraid I have to report that I haven't found anything that I can hand-on-heart recommend, though there are some promising-looking ventures.

For clarification, a book published on the Internet can be downloaded in its entirety or chapter by chapter. If it is web-only, then any sensible publisher will publish in locked Acrobat PDF form (explained above on page 54) so that the text can only be read and not altered. It is then readable either on screen or when printed out. If it is aimed at one of the new e-books (page 77) then it may be in a file format that can only be read by a dedicated piece of hardware.

The matter of easy readability is one I'm going to dodge for the moment (but will return to on page 120) because it applies to other forms of on-screen publishing too. Writers, as well as publishers, need to consider how technology has changed the expectation of their readership. I think we must realise that the general readership growing up today is as comfortable with digital technology as it is with books, magazines, television, radio and film.

In theory, then, an Internet imprint offers a great deal to the writer. Cheap origination and visibility on a grand scale. Does it work?

A colleague of mine, with a background in electronic publishing, turned down a prestigious job because she had a contract with one of the first online publishers on the Internet and wanted to complete her novel (a thriller). She says she would not positively recommend any Internet-only imprints yet. She emailed me saying:

> Promises to publish 'asap' and 'imminently' were not carried out and all manner of excuses were made. The publisher was not responding to enquiries, or to a letter from my agent, or to a recorded delivery letter

which was not accepted. I had to get my solicitor to send a letter invoking the breach of contract clause. They appeared to be the only people demanding electronic rights for the duration of copyright. I argued with them about this at the start, but they wouldn't budge. Most publishers (who didn't exist then) want three years at most.

Feona Hamilton

There are perhaps a number of lessons to be learnt from this. The first is that Internet-only imprints have not yet established themselves; have not built up a profile that is known and trusted. Some come close to vanity publishing while others are genuinely seeking new talent. You should bear this in mind when looking at the imprints listed in Part 2:5 **Electronic origination**, page 171. Check to see if they are members of the Association of Electronic Publishers, who are trying to set some ground rules, though bear in mind that (as so frequently in this and other fields) it is an American association. That does not necessarily matter because the global nature of the Internet means that places of origin may not be relevant. But electronic publishers outside the US who develop a worthy presence may not be members of a US association – this is a prime case of needing Internet-wide associations.

The second lesson is that anyone should be wary of a publisher – paper or online origination – who wants to grab electronic rights in perpetuity. There's more on this on pages 92-4 and 148-9.

The third lesson is that you need to examine the online publisher's site very carefully. Read their guidelines page: see if they have a sample contract online, study its clauses, ask to be put in touch with other authors to gather their opinion. Ask to see their statistics – how often is a successful book downloaded? What's the cut?

Previewbooks – a Canadian venture whose sales technique is to offer half the book free and then charge $9.95 for the rest – offers statistics. When I looked they had been running for one year and their downloads were in the teens or early hundreds, with 'Cooking on the Wild Side' the top title at 268 hits. What we don't know is how many of those 268 people bought the rest of the book. Even if they all did, what percentage did the author get? Say it was 50 per cent – do your sums and ask yourself whether it was worth it.

The fourth message is an old one: if it's a good idea, why aren't the big publishers doing it? It takes many years for publishers to build up a reputation and for their imprints to gain the weight of

authority in a given field. Most writers would
published by a well-known house, but until very
traditional publishers have remained, well, traditional. CD-ROM publishing, as an earlier dip into electronic publishing,
and in certain limited reference fields that was successful. But, with
some exceptions, most CD-ROM publications in what's commonly
called 'creative writing' failed to recoup their capital outlay.
Publishers who had made a substantial investment in electronic
publishing shut down the units.

As a result, traditional book publishers have largely closed their
eyes to the Internet, and how it will affect their publishing and selling divisions. Many of the old-world giants are in denial and
doggedly continue to target a pre-digital readership. It's partly
because a secure and world-accepted charging mechanism is *still*
not in place. Publishers want to make money. So do authors. But
some writers just want to be read.

There are signs that the industry is now emerging from its
slumber. As I write Penguin Putnam is expecting to launch one of
its titles as an e-book original, five months ahead of its scheduled
publication as a paperback original. The book is to sell as a downloadable file for roughly the same price as the print edition (why
not less, I hear you mutter). What is interesting is that the title is a
mass-market one, a Stephen King thriller, and that's an indicator of
how the profile of the typical online audience is changing.

These are early days in Internet publishing and writers must be
content with looking at daguerreotypes for the moment where they
anticipate Miramax circular cinema.

E-books

The book metaphor seems curious in relation to files on magnetic
media, but it is in a continuous tradition. The original *bóc* described
a 'writing-tablet, leaf, or sheet' and is etymologically related to
beech-tree, the suggestion being (says *OED*) that inscriptions were
first made on beechen tablets, or cut in the bark of beech trees. The
e-book is simply an electronic counterpart.

Forget the 'You can't read it in the bath' complaint and all the
other anti-screen arguments – they're all in the process of being
disproved though it will take a while yet because small backlit display screens at acceptable resolutions are still expensive. But

technology is improving and as a new generation of people who are used to reading on small screens grows up, the demand that spurs development will undoubtedly accelerate.

Benefits to readers are:

- **availability**: instant gratification for new, backlisted or out-of-print titles
- **searchability**: terms, definitions and other references retrievable
- **customisability**: modify screen contrast, font size and style
- **portability**: carry a vast amount of reading material in a small package

The benefits of e-books to authors are compelling: much greater control over your own content and marketing, complete copyright ownership and a bigger piece of the financial pie. Most authors receive royalties of around 10 per cent. But with e-books – theorising a 50-50 split – an author might make more money on an e-book selling for £6 than a paper book selling for £20.

That's all very well, but the technology is not going to work until we have an electronic-text-format standard – an internationally agreed presentation format that all hardware manufacturers adhere to so that any text created for one e-reader can equally well be used on another. For example, once the 'A' paper sizes were accepted as UK standard, manufacturers could produce folders that could hold A4 or A5 texts. That made a difference to UK-compatibility but is still a problem transatlantically since paper sizes are different on the continent and in the US.

If we had electronic equivalents of A4 for the content, then we could welcome all the e-readers (equivalent to folders) that manufacturers are developing because it would be a matter of personal preference or aesthetics, with interchangeable content. The nearest we are to this is PDF format, but it is not a standard.

Fortunately there is some glimmering light in the Open Electronic Book Standards Initiative which is working towards a specification for e-book file and format structure based on HTML and XML, the languages used to format information for websites. Authors and publishers will be able to format a title once according to the specification and the content will be compatible with a wide variety of reading devices. Agreeing on a common set of file specifications will allow them to reach a large audience without separately reformatting their titles for each machine.

The Open E-Book Publication Structure Specification aims to provide a base specification for representing the content of electronic books. Specifically, to give content providers minimal and common guidelines which will ensure seamless fidelity, accuracy, accessibility and presentation of electronic content over various electronic book platforms. The technical specification http://www.openebook.org may offer an opportunity to those who can follow its abstruse reasoning, and the non-technical amongst us will just have to wait until word-processor developers create interfaces that incorporate the standards automatically.

Content

For present purposes I am regarding any full-length work that is displayed in digital form as an e-book. But what's full length and what isn't is harder to define now that economics doesn't determine the number of pages a publisher will afford. The Publishers Association at one time defined a book as being 48 pages for the purpose of legal deposit – as opposed to a monograph or a pamphlet.

The sorts of e-books that exist are:

- Full texts of out-of-copyright works. Many are available on university sites and are invaluable for research.
- Mass-market new works for hand-held e-readers – simultaneously with (and sometimes now *prior to*) paperback publication.
- CD-ROMs in text or multimedia form.
- A taster of the full printed book – usually contents page, excerpts and some pictures displayed with links on a website. The idea is that it whets your appetite for the full work and you then order it online.
- Totally new writing concepts such as soap operas (cyber-soaps), collaborative fantasy novels and comics – interactive online productions.

Texts online

Several of the sites listed in Part 2:3 **Texts online**, page 166 offer content for browser viewing or downloading to e-readers. Two deserve special mention.

Project Gutenberg, which was one of the first collections of digitised texts, aims to make one trillion e-text files freely available online by 31 December 2001. They're all out-of-copyright or copyright-cleared, of course. And also a bit unreliable from a scholarly point of view. All texts have been digitised by volunteers, either by scanning or retyping, and although they claim to be proof-read and put through the editorial mill, the truth is that some are and some are not. It's slightly the luck of the draw. So whereas they might be acceptable to launch into an e-reader to take on holiday, you may want to check for authenticity before running literary analyses.

The more reliable Oxford Text Archive **http://www.hcu.ox. ac.uk/ota/public/index.shtml**, by contrast, or the Electronic Text Center at the University of Virginia **http://etext.lib.virginia. edu/english.html** have full bibliographic information with proactive efforts to clean up the texts (and, most importantly, these are documented). Both sites offer texts in electronic form for academic discovery: stylistic analysis, language teaching, morphology, textual criticism, thematic analysis, dictionary-making or analysing non-literary texts in order to attribute authorship to unsigned texts. They make sure their client-base understands copyright issues. But these matters are poorly understood by the Internet amateur community, so be aware, when you come across texts online, that anyone with a scanner can digitise and upload a text and ask yourself how you would feel if it were yours.

E-readers

E-readers are computers as well as book look-a-likes. They add value to e-books by offering search facilities and hyperlinking. Most will carry tens or hundreds of e-books, allow you to change the font size and type (perhaps colour as well), make notes with a stylus pen and look up words in the included dictionary. Some double up as address books and diaries.

The problem with the hand-held e-reader is that the market still hasn't settled. I have seen a number of early versions, starting with the now defunct Sony Discman, which was very limited and uncomfortable on the eye. It was far from a highly developed state of the art. We could compare it to the flicker stage of the early moving pictures. Think how rapidly film and video grew from that.

And though we haven't got all that far, we are advancing. We could be at the Betamax v.VHS stage that once applied to video formats, with VHS winning market supremacy.

Most of the devices described below are book-sized, with paper-back-sized screens. All originate in the US and I'm afraid my viewing of them has been very sketchy because they all hover around the $200 to $500 mark, and we all know that translates to pound for dollar once it reaches the UK. There will undoubtedly be even more by the time this book is published and some of these may have folded. As it happens, two products went out of business as we were reading the final proofs of this book and three others were tentatively rearing their heads.

This market flux leads one to ask if e-readers are really a good idea. The book paradigm seems backward for a forward-looking technology. Besides, surely bookshelves full of books define the personality. How often have you observed that people coming into an unfamiliar room range their eyes over your bookshelf to get the measure of what sort of a person they think you are. Technology needs to find a way of replicating that.

Meanwhile we are offered a variety of devices designed to be 'beach proof' and 'ketchup proof'. And there's no need to go to a bookshop; you download the e-book to your computer and from there to an e-reader.

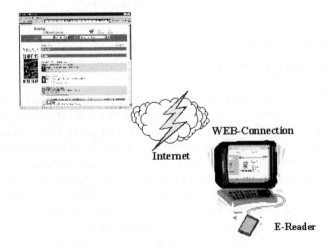

Everybook Inc

http://www.everybook.net

The EB Dedicated Reader™ is the only double-page spread electronic tablet (consequently a bit heavy for comfort). The mass-market version is due mid-2000. The prototype version was for heavy scientific and technical usage (with a correspondingly high price tag) and displayed the work of 17 publishers including McGraw Hill and IDG Books.

Franklin Bookman

http://www.franklin.com/estore

This was a pioneer product in the 1980s (which did some simplifications of Jane Austen for children, if I recollect). The company now specialises in bibles and language dictionaries. The technology is the same as the better-known Rocket e-book (see page 84).

Glassbook Reader

http://www.glassbook.com

The Glassbook Reader is software for Windows or Macintosh notebook computers and other palmtop devices. It is the first in the field to pioneer the Electronic Book Exchange, an open industry copyright and distribution protection system. The Glassbook ethos is to recognise that there are a number of imperatives that the industry must address. Secure copyright and protection against piracy are obvious. So also is support for the giving and lending of e-books. The point for the reader is that economic value of an e-book should be similar to that of a paper book so it can be given or lent to family and friends. The point for the publisher is that there should be only one copy per sale – if a book is given or lent to someone, the original owner's copy should become unusable. The point for the author, like the publisher, is that there are no free copies. For booksellers, the giving and lending must be piracy-proof. And libraries cannot exist in the electronic book world unless there is a lending system.

Knowledge Station

http://www.netlibrary.com

This is one of a number of PC-based e-readers. It's a software browser de- signed to read e-books on-screen, including a Win-dows-based palmtop computer. The e-books are in a proprietary format (called .NKS) with its own inbuilt protection against would-be copyists. Readers can be limited in their ability to print, copy or download an e-book or portions of it. If attempts are made to dis-tribute illegally or abuse the use privileges, access to the book is denied.

It comes from netLibrary and some of its collection of online titles are free (from Project Gutenberg's digitisation of classic works) whereas others come from modern publishing sources. Publishers are not charged for the digitisation of their titles and receive a royalty based on the number of times a book is down-loaded which they (presumably) share with their authors.

There are no charges for viewing the free e-books in the Read-ing Room collection. But copyrighted e-books must be bought – at what seem to be prices equivalent to conventional books. The advantage of that can only be instant delivery. At some point in the future, netLibrary will build a public library collec-tion of copy-righted publications. There will be a small annual fee for accessing this collection.

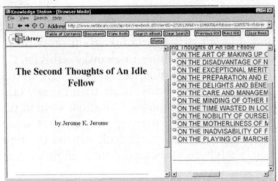

Qubit

http://www.qubit.net

The Qubit (taking its name from quantum physics) is a magazine-sized e-reader, intended not just for e-book and e-zine delivery but for web access too. This works on the cordless phone principle – leave it on it's phone-connected cradle when not in use and carry the robust unit around the house for wireless access. I'd have this built into the supper table so that *Brewer's Dictionary of Phrase & Fable* and the *OED* were always on hand to solve conversational disputes. This would be when phone calls are unmetered and a unit like this one is cheap.

Rocket e-book

http://www.rocket-ebook.com

The Rocket e-book looks the most settled of the technologies. It is a portable device that allows you to download books and maga-zines from some online bookstores. It works via the PC in the first instance and readers then transfer the books they want to take around with them onto the tablet – it can hold 20 at a time. *Adam Bede* and *Angela's Ashes* jostle for attention with the biography of Monica Lewinsky – this isn't a comment; it just indicates range. There were about 1000 titles at the close of the century, more than for any other readers, but dis-appointingly large numbers of them were in the business and self-help categories. However, Penguin has signed a deal with the producers and that may hugely expand the types of available con-tent. Each book is encrypted for a single user, so it can't be copied, forwarded or resold. They seem to be more expensive than the paper editions, which is illogical since publishers are saving on paper, ink and warehousing, but it all goes to show how frightened of technology publishers are.

The interesting news for writers is that this technology could help writers bypass publishers altogether. There is some additional software called the RocketWriter which allows Rocket ebook owners to create their own titles. You save documents as HTML files (easy to do in Word) and 'drag' them into the RocketLibrarian (the software used to download and manage RocketEditions). You could then put it into the Rocket ebook or offer it on the Rocket-Library.com website which is a free taster site. The benefits to the individual writer are unclear, but one could foresee that changing.

Softbook

https://www.softbook.com

This is a leather-bound volume with a writing-tablet-size screen – which strikes me as being like the vegetarian eating nut cut-lets. Why not have the courage to applaud the new paradigm? This is less expensive than some of the others but actually costs more because you must commit to joining Book-of-the-Month club and buying $19.95 worth of books and periodicals from the SoftBookstore each month for two years. It will arrive with 100 literary classics as part of the initial purchase.

The Softbook's one big advantage is that you don't need a PC to use it. You buy books directly from Softbook and download them into the reader via a phone line because it has a built-in 33.6 bps modem.

Softbook has arranged for publishing heavyweights Random House, HarperCollins and Simon & Schuster to provide content for their readers – books and magazines. So the selection should be good. But obviously more limited than browsing through anything from any bookshop.

Personal digital organisers

http://www.palmpilot.com

There are a number of pocket organisers on the market (diary, address book, calculator and so on) with an in-built word-processor which can be tailored to take a range of reading materials. There's a little cottage industry in converting texts for the Palm Pilot and even for the Psion. I experimentally downloaded an Agatha Christie novel to my Psion to read in the Tube train (I take it everywhere). No-one could call this relaxed reading, but it could be OK to fill in an idle moment.

The many texts online from venues such as Project Gutenberg or the Oxford Text Archive can also glide into any hand-held personal organiser. They usually download in plain text and then you can convert the file into a favoured format very easily (run AutoFormat if you use Word).

Handy 21

http://www.lcs.mit.edu

This is a hint of the future – a handheld prototype being developed by the MIT Laboratory for Computer Science to join a television, a pager, a radio, a cellular phone and a wireless Internet connection all in one. It's a new type of portable computing technology based on something called 'communication chamele-ons', software 'devices' that adapt to achieve communication tasks. Not exactly a book size or shape, as yet, but that will surely follow from it.

E-ink and e-paper

All the above technologies rely on further developments because people read 25 per cent slower on screens of inadequate resolution. Research suggests that display technologies offering 300 dots per inch (dpi) will give the same reading speed as print (newsprint is 500 dpi), but the higher the resolution, the more expensive it will be to produce. However, they will have to come down in price because people won't read long texts at a reduced reading speed.

One development is the ClearType font technology, which has Microsoft behind it. The idea is that the 'jaggies' (stepping round curved letter forms) will disappear and the words on the computer screen will look as smooth as the words on a piece of paper. The font technology will use something called e-ink (I didn't invent these terms!) – a dark liquid dye held in microscopic capsules which contain white particles that rise up and become visible in response to an electric field. Thus a positive charge brings the white pigment to the surface of the capsules while a negative charge brings the dark dye to the surface. Intricate arrangements of the capsules allow letter forms to be created. The magnetic charge could be transmitted in a variety of ways – including by wireless signals.

The e-ink and clear type are for use with plastic (rather than glass) screens as flexible as paper (known as e-paper or radio paper), to be handled like paper and even stacked and bound like paper with batteries and a telephone jack in the spine. The paper has the thickness of a business card and the technology is expected to be robust by 2002. Already researchers at MIT and Xerox PARC (the legendary Palo Alto Research Center that pioneered point-and-click computer interfaces) have developed e-paper in prototype form – to be viewed in reflective light with a wide viewing angle. It is flexible. And durable. It'll be more expensive than ordinary paper, but can be re-used thousands of times. There is not yet a consensus about what (or whether) e-paper and e-ink technologies are likely to succeed, but it is an area of interesting growth and opportunity.

Is CD-ROM dead?

It's hard to know how to classify CD-ROMs in this context – you could say the CD itself holds the content and the CD drive is the e-reader. The history of how CD-ROM has risen and floundered in the general market is not one for this book. At one time I did a lot of reviewing of CD-ROM titles for the educational market and I don't think I ever saw one that I thought would stand the test of time. In addition, it always worried me that the cut-and-paste of technology makes study a matter of accessing information on CD-ROM and presenting it back as homework without any internal processing. Teachers call it click-print.

Every writer needs occasional access to important reference works, many of which do exist in electronic form though they may not be available for general sale. The only two CDs I use regularly myself are the *Oxford English Dictionary* and *Encyclopaedia Britannica*. Both are more useful for quick reference than their paper counterparts because of the various ways in which you can search for information. *Britannica* now sells only a minimal number of books, compared with 150,000 CD-ROMs every year in Europe alone. Its most innovative development, however, is to offer the full text of the encyclopaedia free on http://www.britannica.com.

The Internet application of CD-ROM is for publishers to build massive juke-box databases with powerful search engines linking the CDs. A & C Black, for example, has its renowned *Who's Who* as part of the Chadwyck-Healey KnowUK (described in Chapter 7).

E-zines

E-zines are the electronic equivalent of magazines. You can find them on almost any topic. Some are produced by fans, and are the equivalent of a few photocopied A4 pages. Others are professionally produced and can rival glossy print versions.

Virtual magazines have something to offer new writers – possible wide exposure, instant email feedback and sometimes critiquing. But rarely any money. As always, you have to know where to send a story. Some venues are listed in Part 2:5 **Electronic origination: E-zines**, page 172.

And then it's a case of following standard submissions procedures. What is the e-zine like, what are other stories like, how long, are there any guidelines for submission, what is the rights situation and so on? Additional technical matters to establish are whether the moderators will accept attachment files or should you submit the story as plain-text email? Perhaps they'd like you to code it up in HTML.

Newsletters

Also sometimes called e-zines, these are daily, weekly or monthly emails updating readers to changes on a website with hotlinks to the new stories on the site. You can generally subscribe to them on sites that interest you.

E-journals

E-zines and e-journals are not the same thing. E-zines are informal and sometimes whacky; e-journals are scholarly and are mainly electronic versions of peer-reviewed academic journals. Until relatively recently, digital-only journals were not accorded the same intellectual kudos as their paper compeers, but this is finally shifting. Scholarly publishers are also at last finding ways of selling and licensing on-demand usage of electronic versions – though often the consumer is expected to have bought a subscription to the paper journal before being granted access to the website holding the digital version.

Commercial magazine publishers follow suit. *The Bookseller* is one such and, in common with other similar sites, it offers free tasters to lure in the would-be subscriber. Thursdays' headlines can be emailed out to you – and that's a handy way of individual writers keeping abreast of the UK publishing scene without having to pay for a trade magazine they don't want. It helps the isolation of being a lone writer.

There are several abstracting services and gateways accessing catalogues of several thousand specialist and scholarly journals and periodicals. Services are not free – why should they be? The freedom of the Internet ethic needs rethinking.

E-newspapers

Electronic newspapers are generally digests of the full-length paper and do not (at present) offer new opportunities for writers. On the whole, rights to reproduce in electronic form are bought with the rights for the printed article. There's nothing intrinsically objectionable about this if the newspaper proprietors recognise that electronic publication implies higher initial rates, however small these are. Make sure you are giving *non-exclusive* rights and do not assign the copyright. Then you can post the article on another site if you want to. Electronic newspaper syndication is one way in which journalists can sell their own articles again in non-competing markets.

Electronic newspapers are not a replacement for the paper copy, but give readers an overview of world news together with pieces by favourite columnists. Some papers archive all the feature articles and that is quite useful for writers doing research. There is also a search engine that allows you to customise the news you want to read and to search back some way into the archives.

Before we leave the 'e'-objects altogether, look out for another batch, starting with 'e-cine' for ten-minute film shorts in digital video. I'm guessing this will be a growing field.

Electronic publication

Or should it be e-publishing to go with the e-commerce that will enable it? An electronic publication is one that is only available for reading on a computer screen: the electronic component. The publication element ought, in theory, to remain bound by tradition.

Publication is what puts 'authority' into 'authorship'. Unless a work is published the writer has no recognised authority, and is little more than an unknown scribbler. The more stringent the selection procedures for a publication, the more authority is invested in the author. But this is now changing. Today's author has cause to question the basis of selection – indeed to wonder what publication now means.

The dictionary says publishing is 'making publicly known': traditionally, but not always, it is in book, journal or newsprint form. All are publications, the objects that attempt to communicate the thoughts of writers and artists to readers. For five and a half centuries print has been the medium of that interchange and, during that time, different technologies for achieving it have come and gone. Digital print is just another.

Traditionally 'publication' has implied that the work is in a fixed state or final version and is being presented to the world for judgement and comment. The authority or reliability it carries is dependent on the reader's perception of the publisher's public status.

Factual information may alter, but it is a point of honour to produce accuracy at the time of publication – one reason why web pages should always be date-stamped. This used to occur by passing the ideas and information through a sieving system of other professional readers who vet, verify and edit the original. Whether the final form is on screen or on paper should not alter this process of 'editorial gatekeeping'.

What publishers traditionally do is to offer control by promising a level of accuracy and readability (through copy-editing and page design), ease of use (through prelims, end-matter, book design) and distribution (through market targeting, advertising, etc.). They also guarantee the author some payment for ideas and time (royalties and fees, copyright protection). All this may seem obvious, but it is not so clear that electronic publishing (in the first sense of the term as described above) guarantees the same things.

Other electronic publications are in an equivalent state of flux. At the upper end are academic journals published only in electronic form, which are subject to the same strictures as any academic publishing.

In e-book publishing, as in any form of publishing, a particular imprint endorses and draws attention to the value of a printed contribution. Readers take it on trust that expertise on fact-checking, editing, visual presentation and so on have been at work: they learn to gauge which publishers present the 'products' they approve of. A publisher's imprint adds value to the author's work. The Internet doesn't change that.

©yberRight

I said this was the annoying-words chapter. 'Cyber'-everything is becoming hackneyed – cybernaut, cyberpunk, cybercafé, cyberfriends, cyberotica and so on. Its origin, of course, is in the helmsman, 'kubernetes' – the one who is steering the ship. In other words, the authors, artists, composers who are at the heart of Internet publishing content. Some of the practicalities include looking after their rights. But how? This is such a knotty one that I am leaving the detail to Chapter 8, page 140.

I would like to coin the term '©yberRight'. As copyright gives to authors the exclusive right to print, publish and sell their material, so ©yberRight would give the exclusive right to control electronic distribution. We could have a symbol for it – a 'c' within curly brackets, {c}, because computers are currently locked into ASCII as the *lingua franca* and can't all cope with circles. Besides the curls of the brackets hint at the transitory nature of the medium itself, the lack of fixity in those 'lines of light'.

Meanwhile, as users we should be responsible and aware that digital copying is still copying and the fact that so many amateur publishers on the Internet don't appear to know this should not mean we ignore it too. As writers, we should think carefully about our contracts – whether with online providers or traditional publishers.

Contracts

A single word for all authors to bear in mind is 'non-exclusivity'. If you license non-exclusively then you retain the ability to exploit your own work elsewhere. So let your publisher print the novel and negotiate the film rights, if that's what they're geared up to do, but if they are not the sort of publisher who would ever do anything with the electronic rights, then don't sign them away without thinking about it. Contracts covering work for display in the electronic environment should spell out exactly what is being licensed and what is not.

Books

Publishing contracts frequently deal with electronic rights under the clauses dealing with sub-licences or subsidiary rights, though the phrase 'subsidiary' is a bit of a misnomer. Electronic rights are primary rights. If significant primary use is expected, then that will either need to be written into the contract, or the author may decide to specifically exclude electronic rights from the 'for print' contract. Otherwise, they should be discretely covered where the contract agrees arrangements for dividing receipts on TV and radio dramatisation and sound and video recording rights. The Society of Authors and Writers' Guild of Great Britain can advise their members on the general position and on specific cases.

Articles

Freelancers writing for newspapers and periodicals very often find themselves battling against publishing giants who weigh in with contracts or commissioning letters with a great deal of opaque small print, much of it asking for more than the writer is ideally prepared to give. There is no need to sign these contracts or accept inequitable terms; the tide is changing.

Some major magazine and newspaper giants have climbed down. *The Guardian* and *Observer* newspapers did a complete about-turn on their policy to acquire all rights with any freelance article contributions so they could 're-purpose' (their phrase) material via online databases, the Internet and world-wide syndication without paying the journalist any more. They now accept that the fee for each contribution should be in two parts: one covering the original newspaper use and the other agreeing terms for syndication and electronic use. This was a watershed in a long battle being waged by writers' and journalists' societies and the probability is that other conglomerates will follow suit.

In the meantime, you may decide that prudence is the course for you – everyone is familiar with the feeling that if you do not accept a publisher's terms then the editor will go elsewhere to commission the piece. That is an individual decision that each writer faces, though it helps the whole community when well-established writers take a stand against the print conglomerates.

Here are a few bits of ammunition that might be helpful if you find yourself negotiating with a bossy editor (with thanks to the American Society of Journalists and Authors).

Databases supply an electronic delivery system for a reprint service. If your article goes into a database, you are entitled to a fee if someone 'buys' it. The reader generally pays the online service per hit, the database producer takes a cut and the publisher gets a royalty. The only person in the chain who doesn't keep making money is the author – unless the author-publisher agreement calls for sharing the revenue.

Publishers' editors will almost certainly tell you they are not making a profit from the online versions of their print publications. Don't necessarily accept that. They have advertising revenue. There are lots of spin-offs, services and mailing list sales opportunities for the publishers. They gain increased paper subscriptions and general promotion. If the print publication has a website they will tell you a sob story about how much it costs them, yet they pay the web designers, the programmers and ISPs. Why shouldn't they offer a little more for the content to cover electronic usage?

They'll tell you what good exposure it is and that the search ability of the database leads to new opportunities. New unpaid opportunities, in my experience. I got filmed for Sky television as a result of an article I wrote for *The Times* and my editor said the source was 'almost certainly an electronic search – very common these days'. No extra pay, a couple of hours of my time wasted and they never sent me a videotape. You might say, 'More fool Jane,' and I'd have to agree, but it brightened up a rainy morning and was something different in a solitary author's day. They bank on that, and we shouldn't let them.

They'll say they don't know which articles are accessed and that it's too expensive to write a lot of small cheques. That's not true; what are computers good at if not tracking and counting. Organisations like the Authors' Licensing & Collecting Society – ALCS – (and their counterparts in other countries) are specialists in collecting and administering micro-payments and are delivery schemes for collecting on behalf of authors from a variety of sources.

But enough of this publisher-bashing – I sometimes think authors are so fond of this traditional activity that they'd be lost without it. The truth is that the electronic age has pushed authors and publishers into far closer harmony than ever before. They both face a common threat from the lobbyists who think that content on the Internet should be free.

Academic journals

Academic authors are almost always faced with a complete copyright buyout. Scholarly journals claim they cannot survive without such arrangements and scholarly writers have to 'publish or perish' in their jockeying for position on the Research Assessment Exercise scale that now dictates how university staff move from job to job.

Academic authors recognise the need to establish a fair balance between the needs of publishers, learned societies, educational institutions, funding and commissioning bodies, libraries and users, but also feel they have a place in the chain.

The changing technology, however, may demand new business models in academic journal publishing: single article sales rather than whole issues, for example. The tradition of authors not being paid for first journal publication may have to be reviewed by all interested parties.

Electronic editors

Electronic imprints should have the same high standard of editing as their paper counterparts. Would that they all did! This is where brand-naming comes in – organisations who have editorial departments have always understood the importance of good editing, whereas some of the new players delivering electronic content have yet to understand that.

All writers have to be rigorous editors: it's part of good writing. Flaubert used to speak of combing a sentence till it shines. It helps to have a good editor, because even the most alert author sometimes nods. It would be nice if the new era of e-this and e-that would value people trained to edit words as highly as it values graphic designers, who can animate words, or programmers, who can make words rearrange themselves. I'm not optimistic. The economics are against it.

Resources for Chapter 5 in Part 2 and online

6.

New writing opportunities

What has come to be known as a pencil was named because it resembled the brush known in Latin as penicillum. This fine-pointed instrument, which was formed by inserting a carefully shaped tuft of animal hairs into a hollow reed, much as a piece of lead is inserted into a mechanical pencil today, in turn got its name as a diminutive form of the word *peniculus*, itself a diminutive form of the word penis, which is Latin for tail.

Henry Petroski, *The Pencil*

Looking for information is not creative, finding connections is not creative, using dedicated software is not creative. The Internet does not in itself offer new forms of creativity, but an imaginative mind let loose on the creole pot described in this chapter could enrich the language of narrative.

I heard an academic on a platform comment that we are all 'ill-literate'. He and his colleagues, he said, teach their students to 'read the media' but not to 'write the media'. Freedom of speech, he reckoned, is freedom of electronic speech and that means being enabled to use this new, non-linear form of expression to best effect. If that is so, then established writers also need to keep abreast of the new media developments so that their 'literacy' palette expands with the demands of the new century.

The problem at present is that to 'write the media' involves some ability to conceptualise in dimensions other than writing. Already the successful modern novelist is thinking in filmic terms even while writing the novel. The simple pleasure of reading alone is no longer a sufficient lure; it is from the film of the book that fame and fortune spring.

But could there be home-delivered interactive media that will attract revenue streams equivalent to Hollywood movies? Nothing we've seen so far suggests a rush in that direction, but I do believe that, in time, talented writers will migrate to the Internet, once the technology becomes more appealing. And the reader-viewers will follow them.

To capitalise on any initial entrepreneurial concept, a writer may have to join forces with other creative people – artists, experts in music, sound, 3D modelling, animation, computer scripting or games. Someone will be at the hub of it all, like a director in the film world, and it may not be the traditional scribbler. The term 'literary hyphenate' has been coined in Hollywood for double roles like writer-director – should I be writing this book for literary hyphenates?

There is scope for individuals to extend all literary forms beyond their present page boundaries. We should be *thinking* towards a future of e-books on e-paper, as described in the previous chapter, so that when they are here to stay (and I think they will be) then we will be prepared to fill them with innovative and attention-grabbing content. Sooner or later, readers will follow the pioneers.

What, then, of the Wild West as it's charted now?

Interactivity

The notion of interactivity or participation in a work of art or of reference raises the question: is the computer at last giving writers a tool for a completely new kind of creativity? It has already radically changed the way in which artists, designers and musicians work – familiarity with appropriate software is part of their training. No doubt some of the 32 MAs in Creative Writing that exist in the UK (a fraction of those in the US) explore software in relation to narrative, but the new Software Shakespeares are not yet hitting the headlines.

There may be all sorts of reasons for this – perhaps too few writers are interested in operating in a 'for screen' environment; or in playing tricks with content; perhaps it takes one luminary to show everyone else the way; or could it be that there is something inherently unsatisfactory about an art form that, by its nature, lacks point of view.

There is another aspect to interactivity – the transformations that come with the ability to switch at will between media. Watch an opera and click to see the score, or the lyrics, or information about a character, or the composer, how the costumes are made, the design of the opera house, re-choreograph the actions yourself, choose to sing one of the roles, turn off the violins. The technology for this exists for CD-ROM – it will be on the Internet as soon as lows. How do we feel about such personal narratives? has been a means of structuring texts for centuries. It tten forms and also in the documentary (sometimes described as narrative without story) or television news (stories framed by narrative). All are generally in a linear construction, but not exclusively. Interactivity occurs in literature from Sterne to Borges in the sense of abolishing the notion of chronological flow or logical sequence. The advice offered in *Alice in Wonderland* seems simplistic:

> 'Begin at the beginning,' the King said, gravely, 'and go on till you come to the end: then stop.'

There are many beginnings and perhaps no ends in art as in life.

What hypertext offers is one opening and many outcomes.

What is hypertext?

Hypertext cannot be defined precisely: see it in action and the idea instantly slots into place. *The Oxford English Dictionary Additions Series* (1993) offers:

> Text which does not form a single sequence and which may be read in various orders; specially text and graphics ... which are interconnected in such a way that a reader of the material (as displayed at a computer terminal, etc.) can discontinue reading one document at certain points in order to consult other related matter.

It is a term that applies to material intended to be read on screen and the basic characteristics are that text is arranged in chunks of information (like file cards). These are connected by links which are activated by screen 'buttons' or highlighted words. The convention has been that blue underlined words are prompt words; click on them and you go somewhere else. Not everyone sticks to the blue (nor even the underline) convention but you can usually tell where a link is. Each chunk can be connected to several other chunks. Readers choose which chunk of text they would like displayed from the links that are available.

Conceptually there is nothing new about that. A dictionary is a hypertext structure; footnotes are hypertextual. This book is a hypertext too. Although there is a linear sequence, each main section can be read in any order. In addition, the topics covered in Part 1 can expand if you turn to the resource pages in Part 2 and go online using the hyperlinks. So, for example, if (like others) you don't know whether to trust the quality of information on the Internet, see if any of the resources listed in Part 2:3 **Evaluating sources** helps you.

Interactive fiction

Hypertext presents the first cohesive form of interactive fiction though the idea is not new. The oral tradition always made the reader part of the story – theorists now call this 'a personal performance of meaning'.

In hypertext, the reader determines the story's outcome by controlling its branching of events. It is one up from Nahum Tate's alternative happy ending to *King Lear* which was an act of literary vandalism. But more than just an alternative ending, interactive fiction offers an array of 'subtexts' in its hypertexts, bringing fiction a little closer to music in its fugal capacity to express several idea-strands at once.

We use narrative to shape experience and to help us remember. Writers can change direction, vary the pace, repeat sequences and add commentaries, so the narrative can be suspended and altered and may thwart or confuse our expectations. Hypertext does these things too, but replaces the 'shaping' with 'choosing'. It also superficially appears to combine media with which we are already familiar, such as film, television, pictures and books, but the 'reading' or interpreting skills we have acquired from exposure to these traditional media are not directly transferable. The question remains, can we apply what we know about the relationships between narrative and shaping experience (or learning) in linear media to the design of interactive media?

I have to admit to a personal failing here, and that is that nothing I have seen in interactive fiction has held my attention for more than a few minutes – and researching for this book has made me try harder than I otherwise would. Bereft of authorial point of view, it appears to me to flounder, irresolutely, on the edge of meaning, offering little more than a 'white noise' experience. I've not therefore selected an example, but there are some interesting sites listed in Part 2:6 **Interactivity and experimental forms**, page 177. I still half believe that if these forms provide a novel way of investigating a complex topic to give a variety of interpretations, then someday a high-profile novelist will turn to it and give it the popularity it maybe merits. Perhaps that will come when the hand-held e-book comes into its own.

We must remember that the form itself is in its infancy so any insights into it are primitive. When a reader-viewer clicks on a certain word, or set of words, or image, the 'author' has already decided on a range of other words or images that will appear. Pre-programming is part of the form. So-called interactive fiction is a derivative of paper fiction which has long used that capacity – take the plays of Alan Ayckbourn, for example, which hinge on arbitrary choices, or chance, to create many plays out of a small number of possibilities.

Interactive poetry

Poetry, by contrast, transmutes much more successfully to Internet form, being already appropriately succinct. Perhaps poetry is always interactive anyway because the reader creates many personal meanings from a raw and pared-down given.

Poets have been quick to seize the web as a different 'sheet of paper' for a different art form. Within this form, the artist can see the medium as something that continues to control content (though perhaps in a different way) or as one that offers content in which the user defines pathways.

A simple level of control is to offer the reader one verse at a time with button-click access to the next verse. The reader is forced to read sequentially without knowing how long the work is nor having any overview of how it may change form or shape. This in itself makes for a different sort of reading, and one that contrasts, for example, with concrete poetry where the visual shape supplies part of the reader's expectation. Much of the early concrete poetry movement (1950s and early 1960s) ran in parallel to the advertising industry with a similarly productive cross-fertilisation.

The web's ability to add images and video as part of a reading is being explored online. Screensavers are becoming poetic forms which not only present randomised readings, but also offer novelty ways of placing the words to the screen – zoom in, float in, appear left, appear right, with sound effects or without, using different colours and so on. Poetry on screens is borrowing elements from office presentation packages and is looking at ways of bending them to creative effect. The use of such gadgets doesn't in *itself* create good interactive poetry: used by a committed, genuine poet, it can do.

Web-based poetry also breaks down further the already wobbly boundaries between prose and poetry. Some hypertext works, such as *Lies*, billed as a short story in which the reader chooses between truth and lies, seems closer to poetry than to prose (the outcome of the choices, incidentally, remains the same) http://www.users. interport.net/~rick/lies/lies.html.

In contrast to the fiction sites, there is a very rich and varied choice of possible examples of interesting poetry. After much thought, I decided to present the reader with two examples to whet the appetite to go off and explore all the other sites listed in Part 2:6 **Poetry**, page 180.

R.S. Thomas Information http://dialspace.dial.pipex.com/peter. finch/depot.htm is a web composition by Peter Finch that explores the line between data and creativity. The piece contains deconstructed text, found material, verbal collage and original work, along with actual information relating to the Welsh poet, R S Thomas. In keeping with the medium in which it is presented *R.S. Thomas Information* was assembled entirely on screen using the Internet itself as a resource. Here is one section and the underlined word is a hyperlink – don't assume it's in A-Z form, though.

E

emptying earth earth eyes except enduring edge each every even even education earth embryonic ecstatic earth earth ear even eyes equal eyes earth eye ended ewes emerald ewe end earth earth earth's ever embers eye Easter entrance esoteric eyes equinox eira embryo England eyes eyes earth evacuee earth's earth <u>explain</u> eagle ewes equated English eyes earth earth eyes evening eyes eyes encroaching easing expounded echoes eyes eyes earth's expression errors evening enter (stoop) ease eyes eyes eyes earth earth excuse eryr easy earth each eyes eyes eyes eyes eye

Peter Finch

Peter Finch and I first came into contact when we were part of a group of writers who were invited by the Arts and Entertainment Training Council in 1992 to a brainstorming session on setting up NVQs in Creative Writing. An interesting exercise, as it turned out, and one which they mercifully abandoned. Creativity, we all said, is just not amenable to qualification standardisation.

Interested at that time in experimental poetry, he was keen to push at the boundaries and see just how far it could go. It was a natural for him to try something innovative. He emailed me:

> When I discovered the new medium of the Net, I was excited because it is essentially information, data. I reduced (deconstructed) the work of R S Thomas so that it was at first reading genuine, hard, conventional information but, as you have discovered, things do not remain as such. The links (and again I wanted to see how many links I could get in and how many switches and changes a piece would take) lead to either themselves or to other files of real or in some cases fictional information. You can find yourself on a page where the man's books are offered for sale or at a section where his attitude to fun emerges. By now people email their bits of R S Information and I am starting to paste that in.

My second example is Peter Howard's JavaScript Poetry Generator http://www.hphoward.demon.co.uk/poemgen/framset1. htm which readers should try for themselves (and browse his excellent links). He adapted the script for me so I could quote a haiku for this book:

> Young apathy sets.
> A profile shortly stops love.
> Towers bend a judge.

Although computer-generated poetry is not new, its implementation on a website as part of an exploration of new forms of creativity is. Using some rules of syntax and a relatively small vocabulary to generate sentences, the results tend to be a bit surreal, and a bit Chomskyan, but ably demonstrates why we should not be technophobe - writers can mix a new hue into technologies designed with other uses in mind and can extend the colours on their artist's palette.

The web also offers many publication opportunities to the aspiring traditional poet. There are as many poetry competitions online as there are off-line – very often you can submit by email or through a form and readers then vote using software that automatically counts the votes and nominates a winner. The lure is the size of the readership – which I am told is higher than conventional paper-reading poetry people.

Interactive broadcasting and TV

This is a wide-open new area of opportunity, and also of threat. During the writing of this book, Oftel announced the end of BT's monopoly over local lines. Over a period of time, this is likely to lead to an explosion of interactive television and broadcasting through Internet services. These services will also be able to deliver many different channels on one frequency. Current problems with bandwidth, storage and speed of delivery will be sorted out over the next few years. It is thought that by 2006, almost half the households in Europe will have switched to digital TV. Interactivity through pay-per-view is here already via the cable companies; video-on-demand is not far away. These will spawn other modes of interaction.

For those writers who have already written for film and radio, and who are concerned about whether they will see an equitable share of the royalties from these new sources, all these developments can be seen as worrying. For example, it isn't yet clear whether the new providers will act like traditional broadcasting companies. And it isn't clear whether transactional revenues through micropayments and audience measurement systems are the answer. Established broadcasting authors may have to form themselves into action groups affiliated to the writers' societies in order to make new industry agreements to protect any erosion into their rights and residuals.

But writers prepared to be leaders and offer original ideas for interactivity via the web will undoubtedly be successful. Clearly they will also need to be well-informed in order to address the wide-ranging changes that affect writers in these media. And that means following developments in far more than the sketchy overview possible here.

I cannot give you any examples of innovative practice. Other sections may supply ideas or look at the interesting http://www.broadcast.com where you can even listen to a whole audio-book online. Maybe you will be one of the first to think of innovative web-based broadcasting usages.

ve non-fiction

formational content for a web page is not easy. It usually requires the materials to be broken down into small, easily assimilated parts. The practicalities of this are covered in Chapter 7. Meanwhile, what forms present opportunities?

Multimedia

'Multimedia' was the buzz-word of the 1990s and a decade later is beginning to sound almost quaint – like 'wireless' for 'hi-fi'. Originally for CD-ROM, it describes a fusion of computer-indexed information and still or moving pictures with, or without, sound. You might say, that's television, but the difference is that multimedia is interactive. The user has control over the 'reading/viewing' process.

Multimedia combines words, images, sound, graphics, animation and moving pictures linked together in ways which enable the 'reader' to pick an individual path through the material on offer. At its base is a stack of cards of pieces of information which are linked – text to text, text to pictures, text with sound, text to motion sequences. Good writers with an ability to understand the potential of such a medium are still needed.

Multimedia suggests new types of structures: associations of ideas with links that do not supply a linear argument. It seems to work best for encyclopaedic-type materials or historical archives.

For fiction and most other non-fiction usages, we are not yet at a stage where we can judge whether graphic forms of communication convey a level of understanding comparable to that of the written word for depth and permanence. I have reviewed many multimedia 'books' for *New Scientist* and others and I never found a single one that I wanted to keep or even look at again.

Animation

Writing for animated computer graphics is a new art, as yet in its infancy and most fully developed in the games industry – which presents an interesting challenge for the right kind of writer.

The theory is that moving images and dynamic text can enhance the process of communication (just as a good picture replaces a thousand words). This new form of writing for screen reading explores the idea that training can be made into fun and can consequently exploit educational value. It has obvious applications, for example, in technical documentation where animated images might represent moving parts of a machine, or in exploring the flow of information through an organisation. In addition, animation may appeal to readers who are more accustomed to television than books. Animating words requires the designer and writer to work very closely together.

Information chunks

Printed material has so far determined the way people structure thoughts; the way they write and speak. We are brought up in a world of articles and books and inevitably adapt to that world. We stretch and shrink what we have to say to fit conventional form. But now that some reading is done on web pages, which comfortably display byte-sized chunks of text of maybe 175 words per screenful, we may have to readapt. Screen reading may require new shrinkings and stretchings.

Pundits fantasise a world where all published information is stored in the computer and can be retrieved again in small usable units by other writers, who could manipulate them differently to give different conclusions. This suggests an alarming world of plagiarism combined with information overload. If publication now includes chunks of information forever stored in computers, will that leave us inundated with fact but starved of understanding, living in a world where technological progress dominates and alienates us from human control? Data stores somehow point out the gap between what we understand and what we think we should understand.

The word 'infomania' has been coined: an obsession with having knowledge instantly available, at our fingertips. And the fact is that, if you have the online resources, there is a great deal literally at our fingertips.

Who hasn't experienced the symptoms: feeling you're falling behind with what's going on, thinking others know everything? Computer research resources allow us to collect fragments. We get into the habit of clinging to knowledge bits, storing them, linking them, retrieving them and recycling them. This may lead to an undisciplined world of chunks of written information which can be manipulated according to a reader's own priorities: interactive publications.

So far, authors have determined what a publication is. They

have initiated the product: the publishers have transmitted it. We are not yet used to the idea that the receiver might also begin to have a say in what the publication consists of – might mix and match a personal hotchpotch, picking an individual route through the subject material. Survival for authors may depend on being able to work creatively in many different dimensions.

Creativity in a new environment

This book has largely evaded the question of a what a writer is. I've tried to use the word 'author' to describe those who write for book and journal publishing and 'writer' for screen, TV and broadcasting. But it's a rough and ready distinction. Some may consider anyone is a writer when they write. And, as I implied in the introduction, skill with words alone can no longer be regarded as the only defining characteristic of a writer. An ability to create and notate transformations is a parallel skill.

Geoff Stephenson, who is a policy analyst working for the European Commission with a remit to focus on electronic publishing, suggested to me that:

> ✕ Writing in the traditional sense will probably go the way of illuminated manuscripts and plainsong. Revered but not emulated. It may be possible to go much closer to traditional storytelling once we have virtual environments. People will be able to gather to listen to a storyteller in real time or watch a Punch and Judy show. Virtual environments may lead to a resurrection of theatre along the lines of the extravagant mechanical creations of the 17th and 18th century in Vauxhall Gardens, but all in 3D graphics. ✕

He makes the point that interactive games like Tomb Raider and Lara Croft, involving quests that the user has to follow by fighting off monsters and solving puzzles, are the current equivalent of *Jason and the Argonauts* and the *Odyssey*. The generation stimulated by games myths has not yet grown up.

In the electronic arena, the creative input is often spread between text, illustration, film and music, in addition to the programming that adds the interactive functionality. If 'writer' is an unsatisfactory term, how much more difficult to capture the boundaries of creativity as they change to fit new forms.

I think we need to be prepared for change, a change that will only manifest itself over the next five to ten years.

Writing tools

Many writers say that they always do the 'creative' part of their job with pen and paper first only transferring to the computer when the first thoughts have, literally, been pencilled in. For them the computer is essentially a revision tool. Others find they can compose directly onto the keyboard. There are no rules; everyone has their own fads and routines, most of which are privately set up as rituals to get into the right frame of mind.

In connecting to the Internet you will find instant access to new toys for some of the new formats described above. There are sites where you can buy software for screenwriting, story-generation, 3D animation, voice recognition and much else. All are listed in Part 2:6 **Writing tools**. Some, like screenwriting templates or bibliographic software, are genuinely useful because both have formatting requirements – scene headings, action, dialogue, camera action, character names and so on. It's wise to be circumspect. Software won't write the thing for you, yet sometimes people feel they can be more creative with the right tool. We all need crutches. Very often, templates adding-on to your normal word-processor work as well as anything else. Always try-before-you-buy: download a demo or ask for a money back guarantee. Several are free or almost free and that is useful for exploring how such software could help.

There are also some software products for completely innovative approaches to story-telling, such as Alice http://www. cs.virginia.edu/~alice, PuppetTime http://www.puppettime.com, MindMap http://www.mindman.co.uk and others listed in 2:6, page 186.

Part 2:6 also divides into groupings by genre, all pointing at websites that show what other creative writers are doing; how they are starting to act as initiators within which an engagement with the user can begin. These sites are also tools (of a sort) and address writers of various hues – academics, journalists, translators, business writers and so on. These listings (together with those in Chapter 5) indicate a variety of new opportunities.

Tools and style

Writing implements have always dictated the author's style. A chisel on stone does not encourage prolixity. A scroll does not lend itself to indexing. Socrates thought that to write anything down at all destroyed the memory.

In the eighteenth century writers used quill pens which had to be frequently sharpened and dipped into an inkwell; and this led to a leisurely, balanced style with antithetical sentences. By the middle of the nineteenth century the fountain pen had been invented. This meant an author could write for hours without stopping for ink. Hence the discursive style of a Dickens or Thackeray. Then in 1875 *The Adventures of Tom Sawyer* became the first novel to be written on a typewriter. Mark Twain thought his Remington a 'new-fangled thing' and it was blamed for encouraging clipped, staccato prose. (Interestingly, the first typewriter was invented in 1714, but it didn't work because the keys jammed; which is why the QUERTY keyboard came into being to slow the user down.)

Evelyn Waugh thought prose style broke down further with the advent of the dictating machine. Writers could ramble away at high speed in a conversational but prolix way – Edgar Wallace being the prime example. Or have a look at *What Maisie Knew* and see if you can detect where Henry James switched from handwriting to dictating.

Writing styles can sometimes evolve by chance. Consider the far-reaching effect that Proust has had on the development of the Western novel. He wrote the original version of *À la recherche du temps perdu* from 1905–1912. In its original form he intended it to consist of three 400-page volumes. By 1913 the mnuscript would have produced a book of 1500–1600 pages. During this time he offered it to a number of publishing houses – all refused. Finally extracts of it were published in literary reviews. In 1916 the publisher Gallimard took on the novel. But by this time it was the middle of the war. Everything was put on hold and there were probably paper shortages which prevented its immediate publication. So Proust carried on tinkering with the novel, adding to it. Finally, in 1919 the novel had doubled its original length and was 3000 pages long. He was still working on it – revising and adding to proofs as they came back from the publisher, up to his death in 1922.

And a final literary anecdote: Dostoyevski hired a professional stenographer, Anna Grigorevna Snitkina, because he had to produce *The Gambler* in six weeks – reader, he married her.

The point about all these stories of writers is that they were all children of their times and that affected their writing. We live in a time that is flooded by the Internet. Why not welcome it and see what can we do with it?

Writer-in-residence on the Internet

Another opportunity for 'experimental' writers is to find a community site that will fund a writer-in-residence – which is an odd way of describing being the Internet writer of the month, term or year, and just goes to show how stuck we are in the traditional paradigms. The rates of pay are as undramatic as is usual for this kind of endeavour, but a well-chosen site would provide exposure, a regular readership and the ability to work within a community of writers.

There's usually a 'teaching' element, the aim being to bring new writers into the community, to be able to look closely at others' works without personalities and politics intruding too much (which tends to happen in a classroom environment) and to work with others to explore online writing activities in an experimental forum.

My colleague, the scriptwriter Alan Mcdonald, who had an early residency with artiMedia in 1995, notes that it forced him to think about the way that words relate to visual images – the way that words *are* visual representations. He emailed me:

> My simple image of what's online remains that of a slide show. It's like a glorious international slide show, in which any member of the audience at any time can click their clicker and go to another slide, or a slide within a slide. As time goes on a slide can do more tricks – animation, sound – and perhaps this will eventually change the nature of the whole thing altogether, but for now those extras are too primitive to be more than an addendum.

But, he notes, we should all be wary of the word 'interactive'. To click on a word and go to another slide in this slide-show is interesting, but to a limited extent once you've done it a few times. How a writer-in-residence can contribute is in fuelling the creativity of others to form more unusual ranges of work where 'interactive' means that users help to create and reshape the work itself: one of the results is at http://www.poptel.org.uk/unholy.

Browse some of the sites in Part 2:6 **Interactivity and experimental forms**, page 177 to see what's been done and which sites may have opportunities for residencies. Universities and the Arts Council may be open to approaches and Chadwyck-Healey's Literature Online also offers residencies. I anticipate that this will become a burgeoning area of opportunity for the established writer and a source of support for the novice writer.

Resources for Chapter 6 in Part 2 and online

7

Internet publishing practicalities

There are 129,612,000 books in the public library service, which take up 3,600 km of shelving space – or 2.5 times the distance from John o'Groats to Lands End – compared with 3,149 km of UK motorway.

The fifth most popular pastime in the UK is visiting the local library. The first four are (a) visiting a pub, (b) eating in a restaurant, (c) driving for pleasure, (d) eating in a fast-food restaurant.

Statistics quoted by New Library:
The People's Network report, 1997

Internet-based publishing makes it possible for *anyone* to be successfully published. That's the theory, of course, and it's also true. Well, up to a point, Lord Copper, because Internet and non-Internet publishers are all trying to attract the same readers and although it is simple enough to get published on the web, that's not much use if no-one's heard of you and therefore has no incentive to buy your work.

So let's look at the reality, starting with Internet publishing as modest PR (also a form of publishing) and moving on to full-blown credit-card security on a website.

Self-promotion

The World Wide Web is a powerful shop window for your brochure, your CV, a writing sampler of specimen chapters or your complete literary project. It is a remarkable publishing medium. Remarkable because the distribution mechanism is the Internet itself and small or self-publishers are using the same channels and the same media of expression as the large publishers. Advertising and publicity still require skills, but there is plenty of scope for an individual to be successful. This applies particularly in minority or esoteric fields where the author can target (or emailshot) everyone who might be interested in the work.

And you are available to a potential audience of 200 million which is growing with every year. Moore's Law states that power doubles every month, and though that power could reach a ceiling in 2010, they may still become 100,000 to 10,000,000 times more powerful than they are now. Not only will the client-base grow, but so with it will technology's ability to sift and sort material to offer it to tailor-made markets. What that means for *you* is that there is no reason to fear that your offering will be like a needle lost in a haystack. The technology will be able to cope with as fine a granularity as the human mind can devise for isolating and refining the items in this giant-sized database that stretches across the world. And lots of bright human minds are working on this.

As a writer-publisher, all you need is time – more than you might think. There is some capital outlay (beyond the cost of the computer itself) but it is not significant and you can write it off against costs for income-tax purposes. The *quid pro quo* is that the self-publishing equipment itself is a communication centre which has the additional advantage of reducing your postage and voice telephone bills.

Until quite recently, only businesses and academics were interested in web publishing, but now everyone is at it – chocolatiers, string quartets, roller-coaster clubs, pop stars, the Aphra Behn fan-club and so on. Writers are not getting left behind.

Web space

A service provider will offer between 5 and 25 Mb of web space with an email account so that the customer can create a personal website. Five megabytes is quite enough for most individuals. There are also many companies offering 'free' space, and my comments about free email apply here too. Yes, it may become the norm but you always do pay in some form or another. I prefer (and this is purely personal) to pay a fixed amount to a supplier with a good reputation, plenty of bandwidth and quantities of fast modems, reliable and tested support, speed of access and no irritating advertising. Believe me, if there's one thing you can be sure of, it's that a server with inadequate support is down the very hour a potential client, whom you particularly want to attract, chooses to visit the site you have so carefully constructed.

Free web-space providers tend to be (*tend* to be) in cahoots with advertising companies, that's *why* the actual megabytes of disk space on their servers can be free and that is why their commitment of service to the customer is not as great as the advertising-revenue imperative.

There will always be premium services for extra facilities. You pay more, for example, if you want a web address or URL that you choose yourself, i.e. your own domain name. If it is short or memorable, it is easier for people to find you.

You register a UK address through a company called Nominet (http://www.nominet.org.uk and see Part 2:7 **Web writing**, page 191) at a cost of £80 for the first two years. It then costs about £40 to forward requests to the space you have with the ordinary service provider. I acquired http://www.editor.net which is redirected to http://dialspace.dial.pipex.com/town/plaza/dg40 and I think it is obvious which looks more friendly and professional.

Writing web pages

Writing web pages is a new art form that uses writing skills; it is genuinely creative; it requires writers, not programmers; editors with an understanding of old-fashioned editorial values; and graphics designers who understand that readability is as important on a web page as it is on a paper page.

Writing for web pages requires logical structuring, sensitivity to personality and an ability to tailor the writing style according to the medium: the skills a novelist employs. It also requires visual sensitivity. Many writers are used to thinking about how illustrations enhance a text, and novelists must have a good visual imagination – so consideration of design has long been part of authorship. You don't have to invent stories or characters, but plotting, planning and imagination are fundamental.

You need:

- a capacity for logical thinking
- secure language expertise
- some technical ability
- a strong visual sense
- patience
- familiarity with applicable law

If you don't have (or can't acquire) these skills then think about asking someone else to do your site for you

Planning

Writing the text for your website is like any other writing project. The more effort that goes into the planning stage, the better the result. You need to identify your audience, decide who you are aiming at and consider what the website is for. Is it your:

- calling card
- PR brochure
- sales outlet
- information resource
- club or network
- medium of self-expression

The result will vary accordingly. For example, if you just want a simple calling card, then a single screen – what's called a splash page – might suffice. It would have your name, perhaps a photograph of you, a few lines about your specialist writing skills and interests, some titles perhaps, and contact details. The point of this? You can then be found; your personal front cover is on the world bookshelf.

The next step is to get a little suite of off-the-peg web pages by using one of the ubiquitous wizards or templates that will produce some linked pages on the basis of answers to standard questions. Most dedicated web construction software will have a set of templates or wizards (see Part 2:7 **Web writing**). This is an adequate start – though you can recognise pages done like this a mile off, and they are never, *ever* structured for writerly requirements. It doesn't really matter though, because this form of publication isn't fixed in the way we have been used to from print. So you can start with something simple, observe how it works and then change it for a more complex, and personally creative, set of pages later on. Perhaps I should drop down to tiny print to whisper this, it's very instructive to look at the source code of pages you come across that you like and try to emulate them (click on View and then Source in your browser).

Do not go to a web-design house or a Young Thing fresh from sixth form – they are expensive; in love with the technics; and can't write.

Structuring

Even if you ignore the sentence above (and yes, I'm being opinion-ated, but with good reason) you would still need to think about the structure of the site yourself.

So the first thing to do is to draw family-tree-type diagrams with your home page as the great-great grandmother. Give her, say, six to eight children, who in turn will spawn other families. And for 'families', read 'concepts' or 'doors' because you need to imagine your visitor opening doors that lead to other doors accord-ing to which ones they choose to open. It is vital, therefore, to get your labelling right at a very early stage. If you label a door Con-nections, what will your reader expect to find there? Will it be links to other sites? Will it be press information? Will it be a list of rela-tives? Perhaps Resources would be a better label. Or perhaps some people will immediately think of property and assets.

I can't emphasise enough the importance of considering syn-onyms for your top-level labels. How often have you got lost on someone's website simply because the way in which your mind works isn't the same as the mindset of the person who created it? Try and second-guess what a visitor will want in coming to each page and find a single word that most unambiguously describes it. Isn't that what writers are trained to do? An input from the writing community can only have a beneficial effect on the 'grammar' of websites generally. After all, writers have always understood that the point of grammar is not to be regimental, or proprietorial, but to diminish the chances of being misunderstood.

If there is art-work, then the picture too must speak. Make sure its iconography is clear and unambiguous. Remember that when you insert a picture it is good form to give an explanatory note in the ALT (for Alternative) command. This dates from a time when most people turned off images because they were too slow to download so all pictures had to have a text alternative. The text pops up in a little yellow box hovering over the image and presents an opportunity to be more expansive and to headline what's behind the picture.

Once the top level of labelling is in place, you can then sort your information chunks into their respective compartments. It isn't always simple; some things could belong in more than one place. Fortunately the cross-linking goes horizontally as well as vertically and our dreamworld mixed metaphors of family-trees and doors start to break down. In web relationships a door in the attic can open onto a door in the garden; a great-great-great niece can marry her grandfather's sister's uncle.

Confused? So would your visitor be if you let all this promiscuity in time and space be obvious. The initial planning needs hiding in the ways outlined below.

Navigation

If your visitor makes Choice A here, what are the ramifications for Choice B there? Web writing is not static, but writing dynamically is something that most writers have not learned. It is, perhaps, something we will all have to discover as we progress into the web-publishing age.

Branching: Start with a concise introductory page that indicates the site's purpose and then presents a logical branch of choices: 6–8 is generally plenty.

Headers: It is useful to have those top-level choices as a mini table of contents at the top of the page. Ideally, have a button to a site map on each page too. Even better, incorporate a search button on every page.

Footers: Make sure a contact email is at the bottom of every page as well as the date the page was last updated so that visitors always know how to verify the content on the page.

Two clicks away: Each choice should lead economically to what visitors want – ideally they should always be two clicks away from it otherwise they'll get bored and leave your site. This is a good theory, but not so easy to put into practice.

Links: Don't link every prompt phrase that leads somewhere else. Think whether you would like to keep your reader on that page so that they absorb its message before moving on. It may be better to use a right or left margin which gives links associated with that page.

Outside links: Many people like to arrange reciprocal links with others. In my experience, such off-site links are best kept in one place – a single page or folder of pages. That way, you can keep visitors on your site so that, if they do branch off to someone else's, they can always come back easily. To do this, make sure that your code is set to open up a new window for outside links (the HTML is target= "_blank"). Also, there are some unresolved copyright questions where sites bring in another site within their own frameset, thus retaining their own look and feel. It's arguable that the host site is 'copying' the guest site into its own area and therefore plagiarising it.

Frames: Using frames can be an elegant solution to navigation problems, but for the user it's not ideal. Because the page name on the URL never varies, the visitor never knows where they are. They cannot bookmark a particular page, or find it again on a second visit, and that can be very frustrating.

Technical cleverness: Avoid it for its own sake; use it if it genuinely enhances the site. People don't really like busy graphics or background noise – auditory or visual. I will come back to fundamental points about writing and designing for easy reading on pages 120-3 below.

Page sizes: A reasonable rule of thumb is to make each page 35K maximum, because at the speeds that now pertain, anything over that takes a bit long to download. Inner pages can carry lots of pictures as long as you let the user know before they go to them.

Coding

Does writing your own web pages require special programming skills? Not really because you can buy software that 'talks you through' setting up a small site with what are called 'wizards'. As writers, you probably will want to avoid the whole subject of technical code and opt for an icon-driven web-processor program that does it all for you – such as FrontPage, Hot Metal, Home Site and many more. That's fine. They do work. Buffs will tell you that they dump too much extraneous code into your pages and so slow them up. That's true too, but who cares?

That said, those who are technophobic will not find it as simple as it looks and the mechanics of transmitting your pages to the service provider's machines are frequently opaque even to the hardened web aficionado. There may be a button marked 'publish', but to be frank, a dozen or so other things have to be in place before that button will work.

So on the theory that a little technical knowledge goes a long

way, here are a few pointers to make using proprietary web-processing programs work for you.

HTML

All systems employ a coding language called HTML – HyperText Mark-up Language and, at present, this is the lowest common denominator of web language. It will be superseded (by XML); but I do not see writers being at the cutting edge of change. That means accepting that there are still large numbers of people content to use old machines which do not have the disk capacity to upgrade to the posher browsers – even though they are free.

Just as printers used a coding system to translate typewritten text into properly typeset books, the appearance of web pages is determined by HTML. These codes jump readers from one place to another and also describe a hierarchical structure – the title, headings, subheadings, emphasis, paragraphs. It is exactly like old-fashioned editors' mark-up with its convention of As and Bs for headings, underline for italics, wiggly lines for bold and so on. The difference is that you have to turn the code on at the beginning of the specified text and off at the end.

It is often difficult for authors to accept that the coding does not determine exactly how the page will look because font size and style, line spacing, pagination will be defined by each reader's software, screen display and personal settings. This makes it fundamentally different from the book world where separate editions have to be made for the partially sighted, for example. Now the reader decides how the page will look.

Some codes:

<HTML></HTML>	identifies document as HTML
<HEAD></HEAD>	header information
<TITLE></TITLE>	web page title
<!——>	non-printing comment
<BODY></BODY>	body text
<H1></H1>	heading
<H2></H2>	subhead
<P>	paragraph break
 	line break
<HR>	horizontal rule
<CENTER></CENTER>	centre
<B></B>	bold
<I></I>	italic
<U></U>	underline

XML

XML (eXtensible Mark-up Language) is the up-and-coming web language. It is similar to HTML but takes it a stage further and is useful not just as a mark-up language but a data description language as well. You can create your own tags, which means tailoring the data as you want it and the corollary of that is that people can retrieve what you want them to as well.

XML is not a single, predefined mark-up language: it's a meta-language – a language for describing other languages – which lets you design your own mark-up (more on this in the section on metadata on page 136 below). So using the same principles as the basic codes above, a writer could add:

<BOOKTITLE></BOOKTITLE>	book title
<REALNAME></REALNAME>	real name
<PENNAME></PENNAME>	pen name
<COAUTHOR></COAUTHOR>	co-author

and any other granularity of writer-type data. Small parts of publications can have tags – single chapters or articles, single figures or tables, even short quotations. In the long term that will mean each 'granule' of that sort will be retrievable for electronic delivery to a user. There'll have to be associated <PRICE> tags too.

The idea of XML is that it will make it easy to define document types, easy to author and manage documents, and easy to transmit and share them across the web. But not yet, oh Lord!

The trouble is that the browsers – which read (or parse) HTML and XML do not yet recognise these new tags and so don't know what to do with them. XML hasn't become an internationally recognised standard yet.

We're treading into technical territory way beyond the scope of this book here, but the whole question of designing standards and schemas within which XML will sit is something that the writers' organisations are entering into on behalf of the writing constituency. You can see that the repercussions to the publishing industry are far-reaching. Nor would it be sensible for authors to leave it all to publishers to sort out.

Other scripting

This is a book for writers so it is not the be-all-and-end-all of web-page mark-up. It seemed worth intimating the importance of XML because it is going to become a standard and affects writers at a very deep level. Whether you intend to use it or not, it's as well to know a little about it to become aware of the benefits.

As for all the other languages – JavaScript, Perl, the functionality of cgi-scripting and so on, get another book or call in someone else to help you pep up your own site. It's hard enough doing the writing. Putting a search facility on a site or scrambling forms for secure credit card transactions are not to be undertaken lightly. Books dealing with scripts alone have spines at least 5 cm thick.

Writing style for screen reading

If you write for radio or TV, you will have an advantage over other writers. Web writing is a bit like broadcasting: the style has to compensate for the loss of the visual impact of words. Apparently listeners understand only about one-third of documentaries because ideas are not reinforced by their own reading. Broadcasting tries to overcome this limitation by simplifying and clarifying the message. It also uses a high percentage of graphic verbs and adjectives to compensate for lack of visuals. Although the web offers both words and pictures, their very light-switch nature makes them transitory. Graphics rarely support the text – and very often they interfere because of their slow assembly to the screen.

Aesthetics and screens

If only people realised that simple, uncluttered screens are the most restful to the eye. The twirling buttons, flickering panels and ticker-tape messages are give-away signs of the amateur. I was told this in the kindest possible way by a colleague visiting an early version of my own website: do it if you must, he said, just to show you can. And then take it all off. He was right.

Readability

Readability is affected by design and use of language. Book and newsprint publishing aims to turn words into aesthetically pleasing forms – and this has virtually no parallel in the electronic media. Editing and design aesthetics have not been well developed for computer display. Changes take the form of screenful-sized information chunks, with words curtailed to fit into a line, punctuation altered to show up more readily on screen, and phrases added to make keyword-searching easier afterwards.

Nor is the editing and design aesthetic at an advanced state in Internet-based publishing. Top-level professional publishers have learned to use it to advantage, but the new publishing systems put a great deal of power into the hands of people who have had no training or experience in their use. The quality of resulting pages is therefore uneven at best and dismal at worst.

Don't have too much text. Readability studies show that there is an optimum reading line length of, typically, 60–70 characters or 10–12 words. At high screen resolutions, with Netscape or Explorer set full-out, you might get a line length of 150 characters on the default reading typeface. This leads to what is known as 'regression pauses' while the reader struggles to make sense of the text. Invisible tables can help to set the text column at a line length of 12 words.

Studies also suggest that plain white or creamy yellow is the most unobtrusive background. Sharp contrasts aid readability.

Writing style

Many sites are built from documents created for print – brochures, PR material and so on, usually written in advertising-speak whose density is propounded by committee interventions. It's very, very difficult to make those committees see that what they have agreed for print just will *not* translate to the web. In fact the texts need a great deal of editing and much thought. If you are asked to rewrite someone's brochure for a website, photocopy this section and send it to them.

Writing for easy readability is a skill required to reach the reluctant reader. Assume everyone's reluctant on the web – three-minute attention span, and all that. So use easy words and short sentences. As readers delve deeper into a site, so their accept-ance of more discursive reading matter increases. Once they are committed to the subject material, you can write 'normally' and assume they will print out and read from paper.

The average adult spends eight hours a week reading as opposed to 27 hours watching TV. And that's reading from paper. Reading from screens has so far proved less efficient than paper, though with the development of e-ink and smoother fonts (as described on page 87) this may change. At present, however, there are some rarely regarded principles to consider. Take writing for radio or television as the paradigm and then make it even simpler.

Use the tadpole or pyramid structure: Hit your reader with the main points at the top of the page (people are reluctant to scroll). Use interior pages to unfold details and complexity. Have a site map so users can absorb the shape of the whole site.

Be concise: The overall length of a radio or television piece is about a third of a print article; a web page can be even shorter. Cut every word that doesn't contribute.

Write short paragraphs: Paragraph breaks refresh the eye: between two and five sentences is enough.

Write simple sentences: Ideas are easier to digest in a simple subject-verb-object progression. Make sub-clauses into separate sentences. Use one idea per sentence and make them under the 17-word print average.

Use present tenses or the active voice: The web is here and now. Keep passives away.

Use graphics sparingly: Bullet points or graphic elements help pick out keywords. But animations are irritating. Studies show that the message is lost when television images fail to reinforce spoken words. The same is true of the web.

Influence design: Use tables so that the line length is limited to about 10 words in standard browsers. Use white or pale cream backgrounds.

Consider hyperlink clicks: Don't send your reader off in all directions with too many hyperlinks. If you want them to stay with you to absorb your point, put the link somewhere else on the page. There's no need to link just because you can.

All the above is the sort of advice you would expect, though rarely practised. It's not meant to be inflexible. Let's all be careful and heed this warning:

> Today, half the writers I know in this town are either working in electronic publishing or trying to ... Brevity and blandness: these are the elements of the next literary style. I have participated in and in some small way precipitated my own obsolescence. For those raised in

the tradition of linear print, this may represent the bleakest irony of the digital revolution – that we so willingly took part in our own execution.

P. Roberts, 'The future of writing',
The Independent on Sunday, 24 September 1996

Longer texts on web pages

Like many others, I too have adapted longer texts for reading in a web browser – with click links to footnotes or a linked passage and a 'next section' button at the bottom. I now think this is a complete waste of time – laborious and soul-deadening to do, and since the reality of web design is that you have very little control of the appearance of the page, it's 10–1 it'll be hard to read for someone even after all that effort.

Anything over 1000 words should be properly designed in a desk-top publishing program or word-processor. It should be security locked (against manipulation), watermarked for protection if possible, and compressed using Acrobat Exchange (see page 54) or any other widely accepted document delivery standard. Then post it up on the site as a downloadable file. On mouse-click, the file will open up in the Acrobat Reader or the visitor can save it to file and can then print out or read on screen *à choix*.

Writing for digital publication

Such longer texts count as digital publication. For the professional, the matter of payment is crucial. People who write for publication (as opposed to for self-expression/therapy/private chat and so on) have traditionally been drawn in at some level on the fame-fortune scale. A journalist hack writes for money; an academic scientist writes to maintain an academic standing; a novelist longs for acclaim and hopes for large advances. Digitisation and the Internet have changed that – there are growing numbers of people who write and publish digitally with no expectation of gain, but simply because they want to be read. A mutual appreciation of the different imperatives is vital to designing systems that accommodate all interest groups. These groups break down roughly into the three groupings below.

Commercial

Traditional publishing, which for present purposes I will call 'commercial', includes traditional houses as well as a new set of publishing communities comprising software companies, entertainment giants and database publishers. Writers operating in this 'set' feel that whether publication is digital or on paper should, ultimately, make no difference. They recognise, however, that as the creative industry moves further into the era of digital delivery, sole reliance on copyright law for the protection of intellectual property is unlikely to be adequate. What is needed is protection based on technology and backed up by international agreements and universal standards. It's happening – but slowly.

Scholarly

The special-interest publishers represent scholarly and minority communities (many of them learned societies or university departments). The writers do not expect or want to be paid for their words: some few are even willing to *pay* for the privilege. For these authors, the Internet offers a remarkable way of increasing visibility and accessibility and in some areas the cachet of the electronic journal is beginning to be recognised on a footing equal to paper. An attraction for publishers is that publication may be a fraction of the cost, which makes it easier for those writing on minority subjects to be given an airing. The readership of any particular esoteric article may be tiny, but the size of the esoteric serial literature as a whole is quite substantial – maybe around 130,000 periodicals world-wide. To be able to access everything in your subject area free, to have hypertext links to other relevant literature, electronic searchability, to receive instant commentary and peer review, to dream of virtual reality links – all this may indeed advance human knowledge. It is not in society's interest to lock up the free flow of written materials in such a way that esoteric literature goes back into the cupboard again.

It remains true, nevertheless, that the commercial writer and the minority interest writer require some safeguards against abuse by the dissemination process. Any specialist in however small a field will want the protection of paternity and integrity (the moral rights of the British Act that bring it in line with the Berne Convention). It is not just that the academic system is built on author citation ratios, but that (particularly in scientific work) readers must be able to trust the accuracy of the text. With the ease of electronic manipulation, this is of vital concern to the special interest publishing communities. The economic priorities of the commercial writer may not apply, but the quest for authority remains the same.

It is also worth emphasising that the span from commercial to esoteric is very wide and writers have a correspondingly wide range of priorities. The Internet can cater for all of them.

Democrazine

Then there's what I am calling 'democrazine' which embraces a very varied community of people growing up familiar with the Internet, from serious societies to a range of social misfits variously called cyberjunkies, anorak nerds, online hipsters, WWwebsters and so on. They inhabit newsgroups, web pages and forums of all kinds (as outlined above on page 62).

The published product ranges from moderated e-zines to bulletin board postings that are free from all censorship – nevertheless published because they are open to anyone, in the same way that Luther's proclamations were published by being posted on church doors. Some of these Internet venues are very serious; others have the ethos of garage bands, underground artists, cut-and-paste writers. The range is from high-level linguistic discourse to low-level pornography. None of the groups charge for the material they distribute. On the whole, *anything* is fair game. There are signatures on postings (the design of which is a culture of its own) but no ownership, no economic imperative, no control and certainly no authority. This is global chit-chat on a grand scale that has somehow got itself muddled up with publishing. Ultimately we may decide that this is not publishing, but at present the distribution (i.e. publicising) mechanism makes no distinctions.

The home page
Personal home pages come into this category (yes, mine too). They're an interesting psychological phenomenon of self-identity affirmation.

I'm sure it's fair dealing to quote two opening sentences (with their endemic spelling quirks):

> Hi and welcome to the entrance into my house! I have had some graphix difficulties due to a fault in my computer, and that is why I have no graphix on this page. Sorry! I finally managed to get my home-page up and running, so you can visit it now.

> Welcome! This is my web page. It's all about me and what I love. Go ahead and look through it. Currently I have a short discribtion of what I'm like, and what I do. I also have a link page and a collection of my poetry.

These are fairly typical of this interesting new genre in which people present a 'virtual self' to the world. There is seldom a profiteering motive, simply some underlying desire to be noted and assert one's identity in a global setting. It's not qualitatively different from what Plato says (with suspicion) of the technology of books in the *Seventh Letter*: people can encounter your ideas in the form of your 'textual self' without meeting you. But it is *quantitively* different because there has never before been such a wide-reaching publishing medium.

Home pages often get formed into collectives, either by accident or design. In the US (leading the way as ever) there is a Ring of Words Webring (http://www.poetrytodayonline.com/words) which accepts anyone who has a genuine interest in the written word though it does have a policy of filtering out the complete cranks. There are some 1000 other linked sites many of which are aspirant writers' own personal statements, as are the two above.

Personal home pages follow a pattern of the following sort:

- biographical statements and CV
- home, family, friends (pets) and region
- likes and dislikes (media preferences, collections, travel, sports, interests)
- ideas, beliefs and causes (religious, political, philosophical)
- original creative work by the author (poems, stories, articles)
- clip art and quotations (regardless of copyright)
- links to other similar people or groups
- chat zone
- email link

I foresee a growth in this home page culture as the 9–14- year-olds growing up in a Britain, with its plethora of free individuated web areas (40Mb being the space on offer projected for 2001), come to maturity. There is a sense in which all this can be seen as a liberation – true freedom of speech. There is another sense in which it is also alarming because the impetuosity of youth will always be on record. What if we ever have another McCarthy era? Then the archives of home pages could be a powerful political weapon.

Publishing your work on the web

The UK government considers that the Internet has become 'the fastest growing market-place in the world economy'. Its experts estimate that global electronic commerce was worth $12 billion in 1999 and would grow to $350–500 billion by 2002 and to $1 trillion by 2003–05.

Of course, those figures are pitched at commerce, so business people become aware of the threats and opportunities of the future. Any writer thinking of self-publishing on the web is part of that business chain so, unless it's vanity self-publishing or a hobby, it's advisable to be hard-headed about it.

Putting your work online

The mechanics of uploading are briefly described on page 50. I said there that the terms 'ftp' and 'publish' were becoming synonymous. You write your novel, edit it and lay it out, zip it up into a PDF file, post it on a website. You have published it. Now what?

At this point, in a hypertext, I would have two buttons: one marked 'for the committed self-publisher'; the other labelled, 'Well, I'd really like a proper publisher to do it but meanwhile I might as well do it myself.' Let's 'click' on the second choice first.

If the book is published on a website, can you then offer it as unpublished work to a traditional print publisher? This a knotty one. Suppose you post it up and invite comment and feedback, then it is not qualitatively different from circulating work in progress amongst friends.

It *is* different though. At the time of the Dunblane massacre, a photograph of the murdered children appeared on a website for one day only. A parent had given it to the police. The police had given it to the press. Someone had posted it on a website. Like wildfire, every other newspaper downloaded it and used it for their own publications. The school photographer who had taken this picture was deprived of the opportunity of charging a copyright fee on the picture; moreover he could not conceivably sue because it would have been ghoulish and mercenary so to profit. The newspapers profited, though.

Whether or not the photographer would or should have made any money out of such a disaster is not the issue. It simply demonstrates that the Internet is an open postbox available to millions. Technically speaking, you put your book online and someone *can* find it. That makes it different from private circulation.

In practice, I doubt if any Stephen Kings are failing to make millions because of such an event. Publishers would probably not regard it as previous publication. But no rules have emerged, and if there is a chance that posting a book on the web in any format whatsoever might damage the economic viability of other sales of that work, then I would think very seriously about it before plunging in. At the very least put disclaimers up – say it's a reading draft, invite comment, and slap copyright prohibitions all over it.

Selling your own work online

Now we've 'clicked' on the first of my two imaginary buttons above.

The essential question to ask yourself is whether you really want to be your own publisher, typographer, rights department, sales rep *et al*. I own up to a personal bias here. I'd rather concentrate on what I can do – the writing – and enjoy the complementary expertise of others to facilitate the rest.

Selling work online means being your own publisher and managing a website to deal with customers, understanding e-commerce, liability, security and protecting the privacy of your clients.

Privacy
If you capture information about visitors to your site (especially, but not exclusively, information they give you by filling in a form, or by response email), you have to comply with legislation regarding what you can do with that information.

Selling through Internet bookshops
Suppose you opt for a 'betweeny' position – self-publish in print form and distribute through the Internet Bookshop, Bertelsmann OnLine or Amazon. There's something to be said for this as they list every book in print so your book will always turn up on a

search. However, the reality is that while the book may be *found*, it may not be *supplied*.

Hunter Steele at Black Ace Books asked me to order four of his listed titles from different Internet bookshops. He wanted to test the hype at a London Book Fair. One came from Amazon UK in three days, but not at a discounted price (as they promise). The other three never came. Amazon (again) told me three months later that they couldn't supply it. Neither Bertelsmann OnLine nor the Internet Bookshop responded. All three books were under £10 and, as Black Ace explained, it makes no economic sense for a small publisher to raise an invoice for under £10. Additionally, as a publisher, you would have to have distribution agreements with Bertram's and Gardner's, which is where the Internet bookshops send their orders. My friend did have, but it's not so easy for self-publishers.

On-demand/out-of-print

When my book *Writing on Disk* went out of print, the rights reverted to me. That was useful, because I was able to redeploy bits of it for my monthly technology pages. I could not have done that under what threatens to be the new system of on-demand publishing via the Internet.

This is essentially a print service offered by publishers (academic publishers, mainly) so that they can supply single copies without holding stocks or taking reprinting risks. The Ingram Book Company (Lightning Print) machine produces single books complete with binding and colour covers at the touch of a button. All it requires is one copy of the printed book, which it cuts up, scans in and adjusts for maximum fidelity. The digitised results are stored on the server, awaiting a book order.

If this spreads – and it will – it will mean there is no such thing as out of print any more because one digital master is all it will take to count as 'in print'. While this has obvious advantages to the user, it's not necessarily such a good thing for an author. You would be precluded from moving to a different publisher, or from getting your rights back even if there were merely two or three sales a year.

If you are negotiating any sort of contract for a work that is displayed on, or delivered by, the Internet, then you should check with the Society of Authors on what definitions it and its sister organisations have come to about what 'in print' and 'out of print' are to mean in a digital world. A work should not be considered to be 'in print' just by being available in print-on-demand form.

Do also be wary of on-demand cowboys. There are some web publishers who offer this as a service to writers. Some of the ones I have looked at are perilously close to being vanity publishing – I hope I have excised these from the listing in Part 2:5 **Electronic origination**, page 170, but I cannot be sure the picture will not change.

Security

Selling books or poetry on the Internet comes into that activity sporting the ungainly word 'e-commerce' (back to the 'e' words). What's different in this environment is ensuring reliable and secure ways of making payments and protecting computer systems from external attack.

Studies show that one of the main reasons why people view e-commerce with suspicion is anxiety about the security of financial information when paying over public networks. We are all familiar with credit cards. There are risks on both sides when using them; the seller needs to be sure that the card is being used legitimately; the buyer needs to be sure the seller won't use the card for charges other than those authorised; and if the information is transmitted over distance – by post, phone, fax or email – then the security of the transaction is even more of a concern.

Although purchasers routinely send such information in the post or give it over the phone they are more cautious about supplying it via an Internet connection. Part of this caution undoubtedly arises from unfamiliarity with the medium and as more and more people try it without experiencing any fraudulent use of their card information it will become more acceptable. In fact, credit card companies (such as egg) are beginning to offer protection for Internet users.

Internet technology allows secure transmission of such information using encryption. Protocols have been defined which cover many of the concerns which arise when making payments in this way. But it's a bit of a minefield. Not least because buying and selling on the Internet only makes sense if it is global and different governments have different attitudes towards cryptography.

Encryption

The principles of Fermat's Last Theorem explain why encryption is now much more secure than it was in the days when the Enigma machine code was cracked in the Second World War. Encryption works because the decrypting key is the product of two prime numbers and that presents a mathematical obstacle course to the code cracker that is so laborious that it simply isn't worth it. Let's be realistic – we're writers not world-stage politicians.

Public Key Cryptography works very roughly like this.

Your text is reduced to numbers and then turned into another string of numbers with a Public Key which distorts the signal. Imagine you are scrambling eggs.

You then have a private key – which only you and the recipient know and which does not, of course, travel with the document – and this has a reverse signal. Imagine that you are unscrambling the eggs and popping them back into their shells.

Leaving out the technical details, the encryption software gaining acceptance is called PGP (Pretty Good Privacy) and the unique key to the code used is split into two halves. One half, the secret key, always remains on your computer and is used to decrypt messages previously encrypted with the other half, the matching public key. Individually they can only be used for half the process, so it is perfectly safe to issue your public key to anyone with whom you wish to communicate securely. They can use your public key to encrypt a message to you, but only you, with your secret key, can decrypt and read it. And vice-versa of course, you can encrypt messages to anyone sending you their public key, but only they can decrypt them. Anyone intercepting any public key in transit can do nothing with it.

To return to credit cards. Whether you give out your own credit card details or expect a buyer on your site to do so, you must be sure the numbers and dates are going to be encrypted. There are 'sniffer' robots that can hunt out web traffic as it goes from the sending machine to the receiving one and extract credit card numbers and expiry dates. Reputable e-commerce sites will reassure you that the details you give are safe from the sniffers – but it's unwise to give your credit card details in an email, though you could safely send the first ten digits in one email and the last digits and expiry date in another.

If you order anything from a website, you should look for a claim such as this and be suspicious if it is not there.

> To order XXX, please fill out the following form. For your protection, your information is encrypted using Secure Socket Layer (SSL) technology. SSL encrypts all ordering information, such as names and credit card numbers, so that it cannot be read in transit. When you place an order with us your credit card information is captured and stored separately from your order, so that it cannot be read by anyone other than our customer service staff.

As a web publisher, you will also need to find out more about SSL (which uses Public Key Cryptography).

Electronic cash systems

The banks and large commercial concerns have developed secure systems of dealing with moving money about electronically. Internet banking and online software delivery are here to stay and there's no real need to be worried as a consumer. That's because money has been thrown at getting it right. As beneficiaries, though, market forces are against us.

The trouble is that writers really want micropayment systems that will allow the buying and selling of content in very small amounts over the Internet – a page for 1p or £5 or even £50 according to its perceived market value. And there isn't much mileage in that for investors. So although you could imagine a songwriter having a lyric downloaded 10,000 times at 5p a download; it's harder to imagine quite how you would clock up and administer multiple mini-transactions of that sort with thousands of individual accounts. Collecting societies, which currently collect up small fees for photocopying as well as limited electronic licensing, may provide a model for some of the practicalities, but there are still far too many unresolved issues.

There have been a number of micropayment schemes: the MilliCent and Mondex experiments – which were apparently successful but haven't yet resulted in universally accepted systems. There were others, digicash for example, which went bankrupt – a warning sign maybe.

Meanwhile, we are stuck with electronic versions of the credit card swipe machines. Any self- or small publisher with a website can get it credit card enabled (some places to find out more are in

Part 2:7). Obviously, it is costly but it needs to be because online credit card authentication is automatic and doesn't require you to do anything. These are the things to look out for when comparing one provider with another:

- What's the set-up fee and what is included with that? For example, check on the level of technical and programming help that comes with your basic down payment.
- Is there a monthly fee? Look around if there is because there may be a better deal elsewhere.
- What's the transaction fee and does that include the card company's fee? It's better for you to have a single transaction fee rather than a percentage to 'swipe machine site' and a percentage to the credit card bank.
- How do they report transactions to you – daily, weekly, by email or by post? You'll want detailed reporting and don't forget that means time spent checking the reports.
- What security guarantees are there? (See page 30.)

Economic imperatives

As I said in my introduction, I believe in books and that is why this is in printed form and only the resource file and updates are available on the Internet. But it is also because A & C Black asked me to write it and their expertise (and mine) is in traditional publishing.

I am sure a micropayment system for writing downloaded from the Internet is possible and will work one day, but it isn't tried and tested yet. Writing is hard work and people who write for a living do need a fair economic system. The Internet was too anarchic in its infancy and the 'free' culture that sprang up around it is only slowly dissipating.

Consider this.

At the time of the infamous Starr Report (1998) on the Clinton affair, it could be ordered through the Internet for $4.79, but to download all of its 1.46 Mb cost no more than a telephone connection. It was also more convenient online because of its hypertext footnotes. The print publication charge presumably reflected some other sort of added value.

So 20 million Americans downloaded the online version in the first few days. At a charge of 50 cents per section downloaded, the

$40 million spent on the investigations could have been recouped. This is an interesting statistic for e-commerce in publishing, even if this is something of a special case.

One way in which authors and publishers can use the web is to expand the scope of the printed book – as we are doing (I hope) with this one.

Sales models

Although this section is aimed primarily at small and self-publishers, it's worth peeping at the top end just to see what the paradigms are.

Database publishing

Chadwyck-Healey specialises in high-class databases of works. Literature Online and KnowUK are two models of the way in which purchasing content over the Internet is likely to go in the future. The legal, medical and pharmaceutical industries have long been profiting from highly priced database publishing and it is only very recently that arts-based products have been developed.

Literature Online http://lion.chadwyck.co.uk is a fully searchable library of over 260,000 works of English and American literature, overseen by an academic advisory board. It has licensed in-copyright works which means it scores over other libraries of literature (Part 2:3 **Texts online**) but at a price that few libraries can afford.

KnowUK http://www.knowuk.co.uk provides key information about the people, institutions and organisations of the United Kingdom: *Debrett, Hansard, The Army List, Titles and Forms of Address, Who's Who* and 30–40 other licensed copyright volumes. It is aimed at library organisations with licences averaging £2400 – well outside the range of the individual. More economic school licences will start in early 2000 and there are plans to expand to home use eventually. For most people, a trip to the library or waiting for the annual Learning at Work day every May (when it will be free) must suffice.

I suspect the future of online publishing is in collections like KnowUK (and KnowEurope) with sophisticated search mechanisms carving a path through multi-information. A colleague arranging a literary festival wanted to target famous people with an interest in chess; a task relying on luck with paper reference, but reduced to minutes online.

To return to the various possibilities of self-promotion, what sales pitches can the writer (published or self-publishing) aspire to? And just for the sake of adding value I'll take a few examples of books with an electronic writing theme.

The appeal to honesty

The Virtual Community by Howard Rheingold (denizen of one of the first communities called The Well) is a book about communities online and (in the true spirit of sharing) it *is* online, in 12 sections http://www.rheingold.com/vc/book. The author recognises the dilemma in his opening sentence:

> Note to readers: I can see that thousands of people are reading or at least looking at each chapter of this book every month. Excellent! I put these words out here for the Net without charge because I want to get as much good information distributed as possible right now about the nature of computer communications. But I am also competing with myself. HarperCollins' paperback edition pays me about a dollar a book. So if you like what you read online, go out and buy a copy of the ink-and-dead-trees edition and give it to someone who needs to read this.

In response to the query as to whether this appeal works, Howard Rheingold emails: 'I have no figures, actually. Frankly, commercial considerations were not my motivation. There has been so much bad information about the Internet that I felt a duty to make good information available.'

Try-before-you-buy

Digital Aesthetics http://www.ucl.ac.uk/slade/digita is an academic writer's loss-leader promotion; see if it provokes ideas.

> WELCOME to the Digital Aesthetics site, a companion to the book of the same name, written by Sean Cubitt and published by Sage in London and New York in 1998. Because of constraints on price, the book had no illustrations, so one purpose of the site is to provide images discussed in the book. But there is more. Four years of research went into the final 80,000 word manuscript, of which about 6 months was spent cutting materials. This site provides outtakes from that editing process, sections, essays and parts of chapters cut for reasons of space.

Onsite is a contents page and ordering details for the book itself and enough of a flavour of the book for those tempted by the specimen chapters – or in this case by the extra chapters that did not fit – to try before they buy. The book's author admits that this style of offering samples can be regarded as a loss leader, emailing me: 'First they indicate something of the style and content to allow potential readers to size up the book. Second they indicate some special interests which have resulted in further commissions.'

Not-for-profit

Professor Mike Sharples is an academic writer who takes the view that being a published author is not necessarily the best way of achieving the recognition and respect of your peers. A helpful, thoughtful or provocative website, he says, can do more to boost a reputation than any number of worthy monographs. He and his publisher (Routledge) agreed to produce a site for his book which adds value http://www.routledge.com/routledge/rcenters/linguistics/sharp.html.

There is a contents listing and an essay on the conundrums posed by writing a book in an electronic age. After 20 years of effort by visionary researchers and the world's major companies the electronic book *still* isn't with us in an affordable form or generally accepted format. (See Chapter 5, pages 80-7 for an overview of the variations.)

Most book sites offer a contents list to whet the buyer's appetite with something extra so you want to read on. The first few pages of a novel might do very well with a click button inviting readers to download or order the rest of the book then and there.

Metadata

Metadata has come up a few times in this book already. It is often described as 'stuff about stuff' or 'data about data' because it provides basic information such as the author of a work, the date of creation or links to any related works. It is not a new concept, simply a new term to describe familiar types of information like bibliographic records or price barcodes. Because all electronic commodities can be described as 'data', all data about electronic commodities are 'metadata', and the word has been extended in practice to include data about non-electronic 'creations'.

It should (ultimately) be good news because it will provide a way of cataloguing the Internet. That means all those fruitless and irrelevant searches will whittle down to what you actually want.

The idea is to define content on websites by using metatags so that information may be more easily retrieved by users.

A metatag is a unit of information that is embedded into the code (customisable with the new functionality promised by XML). Although the user of the web page cannot see the metatag, the machine accessing the code can. In this way search routines can look for documents based on their description. The heart (or should I say core) of much library activity in this area is Dublin Core and its basic metatags are:

TITLE: The name given to the resource by the CREATOR or PUBLISHER

CREATOR: The person or organisation primarily responsible for creating the intellectual content of the resource

SUBJECT: Keywords; controlled vocabulary; classification

DESCRIPTION: A textual description of the content of the resource

PUBLISHER: The entity responsible for making the resource available in its present form

CONTRIBUTOR: A person or organisation not specified in a CREATOR element who has made significant intellectual contributions to the resource

DATE: The date the resource was made available in its present form

TYPE: Category of the resource

FORMAT: Data representation of the resource

IDENTIFIER: String or number used to uniquely identify the resource

SOURCE: Unique string or number for a printed or digital work from which this resource is derived

LANGUAGE: Language(s) of the content of the resource described

RELATION: The relationship of this resource to other resources

COVERAGE: Spatial and/or temporal characteristics of the resource

RIGHTS: Link to a copyright notice, etc.

As you can see, the list reads like a traditional card catalogue entry found in any library. And note that there is a creator's tag which is very significant indeed for the future of writers on the Internet. The World Wide Web Consortium, a group that is concerned with the standardisation of information on the Internet, fully endorses the idea of a set of metatags, though their exact description will not be decided in time for the first publication of this book. It is likely to allow other sets of tags – also known as identifiers – that describe people, things and their relationships.

People (and for us that means writers as creators) need to be uniquely identified because e-commerce depends on being able to track who they are and what they are entitled to. These identifiers will almost certainly be numeric.

The most successful of these to date is probably the CAE – Compositeur, Auteur, Editeur numbering system which is the basis of international royalty management among the European and American copyright societies. (Readers who are registered with the Authors' Licensing & Collecting Society will all have a CAE number.)

Once there is a consensus, and web designers and publishers routinely use metatags and unique identifiers, then search engine interfaces will be modified to look and act more like library catalogues. Users will have the option of doing keyword and subject searches, as well as searching by any of the metatags – the writer's name, for example. Once the Internet has easily retrievable content then it really will feed the Information Age.

Maintenance

The rule of thumb recommendation is to allow two-thirds of your budget in launch construction and one-third in first year maintenance. Ideally, try to design a site where some pages can be left relatively static whereas others are maintained on a weekly or monthly basis. It is also good practice to date-stamp each page so visitors know what is current and what is archival. E.g. it is vital to know:

WARNING: For Archival/Historical Interest – This document dates from 1995 and has not been updated

The importance of maintenance cannot be over-emphasised. Three months is a long time in electronic publishing and, unless pages that need to be constantly reviewed are kept up-to-the-minute, there is little point in the large initial expense of web publishing even if that expense is your own time.

Web publishing is time-consuming. It's not for everyone. But the real plus is that there need not be a publication deadline. It can always be up to date.

Resources for Chapter 7 in Part 2 and online

8.

Issues in an online environment

Where is the Life we have lost in the living?
Where is the wisdom we have lost in knowledge?
Where is the knowledge we have lost in information?

T S Eliot, 'Choruses from "The Rock"'
from *Collected Poems from 1909-1962*

This is the 'but stay thy hand' chapter. If you've been reading this sequentially, you will have noticed a progression going from the basics of Internet connectivity to a moderately optimistic hype on the new writing opportunities it affords. Now for the Luddism and heart-searching.

Anxieties and concerns surrounding the digital age have spawned quantities of books and philosophical debates. People are, with good reason, concerned about questions of: democracy, access, censorship, privacy, liability, rights management, cultural imperialism, audience manipulation, violence and pornography, pop culture, quality control, voyeurism, oralcy and media, information overload, information v. knowledge, Press ethics, English-language dominance – the list is endless.

It is also not a new list. These wide subjects have been occupying us since ancient times. They just have a new spin on them, that is all. Nor need we examine each one. These are emotive concepts and any reader can see how the Internet's lack of boundaries – its easy virtue and ubiquitousness – make matters like the instant availability of online violence and pornography a different kind of concern from their existence in a closed and access-controlled environment. But let's leave that to the politicians and the net-nannying software consultants. Our concern in this book is uniquely with how this environment is different *for writers* from what existed before the digital age.

Those differences merit a whole book, not just a chapter, but that book can't be written yet because so many of the legal issues that could radically alter its tone are still up in the air, and likely to remain so over the duration of the first edition of the present book. So I will distil them down to just those areas that writers really need to be aware of: aware because in the first years of this new century writers' action groups will use their influence for the benefit of the whole writing community. After all, the publishing business continues to move into the hands of the merger-happy mega-firms. Authors can only pull their weight if they merge too.

Writers and ownership

In one sense, not much has altered. The Internet may defy boundaries and bring with it a free-for-all culture, but we're still an age concerned with ownership. Our whole culture is based on it.

The ownership story for writers begins in England with the Statute of Anne of 1709, the world's first act protecting publishers' rights. Its forerunner, by almost half a century, was the deeply flawed Licensing Act, which made it illegal to publish anything without first securing a licence from the 'appropriate authority' – much criticised, since such control inevitably lead to censorship, and it is interesting to remind ourselves of this in the light of developments that may be putting service providers in a similar position. When this act came up for renewal in 1693, the House of Lords dissented, speaking for the first time of the 'properties of authors'. This confirmed the identity of the writer not merely as creator, but owner as well, and laid the foundations of protection that continues into the electronic age.

British writers such as Milton, Locke, Defoe, Addison, Pope and Dr Johnson wrote at length on the importance of literary ownership as did their counterparts abroad. Defoe, in patriarchal style, wrote:

> A Book is the Author's Property, 'tis the Child of his Inventions, the Brat of his Brain; if he sells his Property, it then becomes the Right of the Purchaser; if not, 'tis as much his own, as his Wife and Children are his own – But behold in this Christian Nation, these Children of our Heads are seiz'd, captivated, spirited away, and carried into captivity and there is none to redeem them.
>
> *The Review*, 2 Feb. 1710

Plus ça change! We no longer expect to own wives and children, but we are as concerned with property and with child-stealing (plagiarism, from the Latin *plagiarius* a kidnapper) as ever.

What's different now, then? The difference is the extent and volume of the possible theft. We now have a combination of tools – the Internet, the computer and all the search and retrieval tools that go with it – that represent the greatest opportunity for theft ever invented. Anyone can break in and steal with consummate ease from any civilised country in the world (some autocracies do not allow Internet access). Having then got a master copy of a document, anyone can manufacture duplicates of equal and identical quality. No previous technology has ever offered that.

Copyright

I introduced the term ©yberRight in Chapter 5 – as an Aladdin-like 'new lamps for old' concept. Some people feel copyright isn't appropriate to the Internet. At the moment, and for the time being, it's all we've got. Copyright is a right whether the work appears on paper, on screen, on film, over radio waves or just spoken or performed across a room. So electronic words are protected by copyright as soon as they are written and at all stages of being copied on to disks, retrieved from disks or transmitted from any kind of host computer to any receiving computer. In one sense, new technological methods of writing and publishing change nothing.

But it isn't as simple as that. Developments in the kinds of power technology gives in manipulating texts, music and pictures are moving faster than our capacity to find ways of coping with the ever-widening area of possible infringements. I've heard the problem described as 'an exercise of the magnitude of re-arranging the deck-chairs on the *Titanic*'.

There is a triangle of interests that need reconciling:

- **Creators, publishers and producers** must have the confidence to continue to create and produce. Payment for content is not appropriate in every environment – academic authors, for example, may have different wishes vis-à-vis remuneration from commercial authors or artists. But payment should be made possible where it is required.
- **Intermediaries** (and that includes Internet service providers) must have legal certainty concerning their liability for material transmitted by them.

• **Consumers** require the knowledge that they can enjoy rights-protected creations free from onerous conditions. It should be fair and easily administered.

All points of view need to be expressed and catered for. That is happening and in a relatively non-confrontational manner, though compromises in all possible circumstances will take many years to negotiate.

The provisions of the new EU Directive on Copyright and Related Rights in the Information Society should straighten out what forms of digital copying are allowable, and which are not, but it is not likely to be enacted before 2003 or 2004 (updates at http://www.patent.gov.uk/dpolicy/infosoc1.html).

Electrocopying

Storing text or art-work on the computer creates a copy – just as it would be if it were on a piece of paper. Reproducing from paper is photocopying: reproducing by fax, email, copying to disk, scanning, downloading, caching, printing from screen and CD-ROM capture are all electrocopying.

In fact, it's a complete minefield and, rather than list all the things a user shouldn't really be doing under current laws, it might be more forward-looking to say that EU Directive on Copyright and Related Rights in the Information Society aims to sort out some of the conundrums. Although the legalese looks very off-putting, the intention is to make it easier for everyone to comply with the law.

For example, I mentioned in my Introduction the E M Forster story 'The Machine Stops', which I found on two websites. One took it off in response to a gentle RightsWatch enquiry I made; the other didn't reply. But I had made copyright-infringing copies just by stumbling across the story and therefore having it on my screen. I had also, unintentionally, stored it since the two copies of the story sat in my cache for three weeks. It obviously makes no sense to be punitive about such errors.

But that's the user perspective again. For creative people whose economic and moral rights may be under threat, uncontrolled electrocopying is a serious challenge because it provides a powerful tool that has never before been available to an individual owning relatively inexpensive equipment. It enables someone to cut, paste and anthologise. The person copying may fulfil all the functions of a publisher and therefore produce material which relies on the skill and creativity of others without acknowledging or rewarding them.

Photocopying, by contrast, almost always betrays its origin, does not offer much scope for altering and merging material, and standardly produces copies that are less convenient to handle than the originals. Xerography can be (more or less) contained by licensing agreements. But electrocopying offers the possibility of creating permanent stores of materials which can be reproduced in different forms to the originals, amended, altered and in composite forms – without authority.

The problem for the publishing industry (in the process of being resolved) is to sort out what 'controlled' electrocopying would be? Logically it implies setting up a massive policing system with full-time staff whose sole task is to look out for infringements and bring actions against them. The music industry does this already and even though a great deal must, inevitably, slip through its fingers, the publicity does act as a deterrent. However, the huge expense of such policing makes it unlikely in the book or periodicals world. In addition, the sheer difficulty of proving an infringement, where you might have three copyright holders supplying raw material for one paragraph or one photograph, is a disincentive. That is why rightsholders are treading warily and licensing piecemeal.

Fair dealing

Everyone seems to have a different interpretation of what counts as reasonable to copy or quote for the purposes of academic criticism, private studying, homage or parody. Fair dealing can't ever be clear-cut. In the music industry, for example, a distinctive sound or a few notes strung together count as a substantial part of a work for which copying permission is required. Try lifting the first four notes of a Fifth Symphony from a modern Beethoven and you'll have his sound-sampling bravo knocking on your door for compensation.

Writers aren't quite in that league and generally like quoting from each other. What they do not like is for people to help themselves liberally to their work and pop it on their websites. Let's return to the Forster story – because it is typical of what happens on the Internet. The person who removed the story after I'd enquired about permissions had perfectly understandable motives. His domain name was chosen in honour of one of the characters in a story he had always admired and he wanted to explain why:

> I hope no-one feels any damage has been done – my only intent has been to draw attention to what I think is an important story by a great writer. I was motivated in large part by my inability at the time to get my hands on a copy of the story in print, and had the (vain?) hope that if more people were aware of the story there might eventually be enough demand to generate a re-printing.
>
> Michael Wright

Put like that, you cannot help wondering who gains by its removal.

He did remove it, though, and was last heard of contacting the estate for permission. He did not dismiss my email – as I suspect the other site containing the full text did – with the 'information wants to be free' argument (as if information had feelings).

There is no legal definition of what constitutes fair dealing. It is also different from library privilege, though for convenience's sake only, the two activities are often considered together. The guidelines are very roughly:

Purpose: The purpose of the copying *must* be for research or private study of individuals, for reporting current events or for criticism or review.

Quantity and quality: Users may not copy the whole of a book, poem, electronic publication, electronic journal or website, or any other work. The exact proportion of a work they *can* copy depends on whether it is a substantive part of it or not. The print model allows one article from a journal, one chapter of a book, or 10 per cent of another work as a standard of 'fairness', but this is not thought to be reasonable in the digital world. On the other hand, no-one is saying what is fair.

Abstract: It is not fair dealing to copy a whole abstract as this may represent the whole substance of the work. Doing a précis in your own words *is* allowable.

Copies: Only single copies are permitted. Multiple copying always requires permission – though printing a paper copy from a screen copy would not be seen as two copies (even though it *is* logically). Copying the original to a friend is not permitted (posting on a website being a form of copying too).

The 'free' ethic

The 'information wants to be free' argument is deeply damaging to writers. Remember Gresham's Law? The one based on the observation that 'bad money drives out good'. If two coins have the same nominal value, but are made from metals of unequal value, the cheaper will tend to drive the other out of circulation.

If information is available free then it will drive out the information that carries a fee. There's an implied assumption in the section on search engines above, that readers will be seeking out free resources before they're willing to pay for them. We've already seen the Gresham's Law effect. The *Electronic Telegraph*, which was one of the first online newspapers, tried to charge for access: it gave this up as the others followed suit and used advertising as alternative revenue. Scholarly publishers tried to offer web access only to patrons who bought subscriptions. Now they have partially capitulated and offer loss-leader articles and past-sell-by-date items free, with password-protected areas for those who've paid. But pornography purveyors charge for content and have got round Gresham's Law (unless you take the view it's bad money that needs laundering anyway).

Do we then have two possible models? Capitulate to the 'free' content requirement of the ordinary users and allow certain sorts of content to be free at the point of delivery while making sure content-providers have a share in any advertising revenue? Or, do we find ways of adding value so that the users will *want* the content enough to be prepared to pay for it? I foresee both models co-existing. As writers, however, we must make sure that free at the point of delivery to the user does not mean free at the point of delivery into the publishing mechanism.

Plagiarism and manipulation

Technology – and nothing more so than the Internet – provides effortless ways of pouring other people's ideas and expressions into your own computer. Once lodged on hard disk, cuttings can be neatly subject-sorted, keyword-searched, text-retrieved and amalgamated.

At that point, control of the text passes into the user's hands – and it's the huge potential for manipulation, recycling and re-ordering that makes digital texts more vulnerable than their print counterparts. Electronic words, detached from their contexts and comfortably sitting on your own screen, begin to feel like your own, don't they? And the cut-and-paste power of the word-processor encourages that illusion of ownership. It is difficult to regard electronic words as property because they appear insubstantial. It is difficult to realise that unauthorised cutting and pasting is theft.

Yet, as any self-respecting deconstructionist will tell you, any text is the product of other texts. All we are doing is what writers have always done: scribbling away, using, echoing, adapting, pointedly ignoring, plagiarising our predecessors. Much as we might wish to footnote every glimmer of a thought and acknowledge its source, it would be doing the reader no favour, as the footnotes would be bulkier than the main text. Anne Faidiman shows how difficult it is to follow the main argument in her witty essay, 'Nothing New Under the Sun' (*Ex Libris*, Penguin, 1999).

In any case, pastiche, parody and homage are basic tools of the trade. Authorship and originality are relatively new concepts, and until the eighteenth century, at least, such distinctions were blurred: nobody then subscribed to the idea that a work of art was a single, unified entity. Handel was not alone in scooping up any number of previously existing works (by himself or others) and refashioning them according to the needs of his latest operatic commission.

Yet when Martin Amis felt that characters, bits of plot and well over 50 passages from *The Rachel Papers* had been duplicated in Jacob Epstein's novel, *Wild Oats*, he claimed that Epstein must have had his book 'flattened out before the word-processor'. Whether that was or was not the case, even that amount of typing labour suggests a consciousness of copying which is no longer applicable as electronic copy-paste seeps its way across literature.

To some extent, technology can be used to provide solutions to the problems it is creating. Suppose every time someone copied a chunk of digital text, it pasted an indelible name or numeric identifier alongside the block-copied text, even if the user then rearranged the words – gummed to the original like the lettering in a stick of rock, as my friend Chris Barlas would say. Wouldn't that make people less Edit-menu trigger-happy?

Watermarking and encryption would make that a possibility. Algorithms to encrypt digital information already exist, but standards and widespread acceptance of this as a practice do not. Interestingly, the graphics package Photoshop, in its latest versions, has watermarking functionality – none of the word-processor packages have it on the menu bar.

There'll always be hackers who can get round anything that technology makes possible – and in any case plagiarism is a human activity that has always existed and always will. What is it anyway? I always come up with these quotes which say it all:

'Copying from one source is plagiarism, copying from two is research.'

Wilson Mizner

'A good composer does not imitate, he steals.'

Stravinsky

Societies for writers

All the above ownership issues face the writing profession. Naturally enough, writers, as providers, have grouped themselves into organised societies. This is not simply to protect their professionalism, but because the business of writing is part of a very profitable world-wide industry. Digitisation which dematerialises books, magazines, periodicals and so on, is seen by governments as leading to a profitable reality. Writers expect to share in that profitability. Their professionalism has ensured that they have a voice on government-level panels masterminding systems on the global information networks. They need to be on those panels for the sake of a continuing healthy society.

In recent years, British writers' organisations have been devoting time and effort to unravelling the complexities of electronic content and delivery. The writing community ideally wanted a standard contract which could be used as a blueprint for every situation in electronic publishing (similar to the Minimum Terms Agreement for books and the Minimum Basic Agreements for film or television).

At present, however, contracts used for books, newspapers, film and television do not deal adequately with electronic rights. These are more often than not bundled up with subsidiary and ancillary rights without proper attention being paid to their potential value.

At the same time, new contracts are being drawn up for the increasing number of writers who are writing directly for electronic publishers and producers and there are few good-practice paradigms.

There turn out to be so many variables – diversity of electronic products, types of use, numbers of contributors, encryption, payment systems – that simple blueprints cannot be designed.

All writers, whatever their area of activity, should try to ensure that they:

- do not assign copyright if it can be avoided
- reserve electronic rights or grant options unless the publisher or producer can demonstrate an ability and/or intention to exploit them to the writer's benefit
- negotiate terms according to the project in hand
- require the publisher/producer to protect the integrity of the work (and format in the case of screenwriters)
- have the right to be identified as the author
- have rights of approval over any aspects of the final work so that nothing is prejudicial to their reputation

Writers are best advised to join societies such as ALCS (the Authors' Licensing & Collecting Society), the Society of Authors and the Writers' Guild of Great Britain. I was in a working party with all three to formulate the above principles some years ago; they haven't changed. These organisations are working together with the journalists' and academic unions to secure the best deal for writers in an environment that has a very strong user lobby. Their websites are listed in Part 2:8.

Our deconstruction democracy

Computers are widely regarded as a democratising influence because they enable the breaking down of control (the first time of note being when the news from Tiananmen Square spread to the West via email at a time of stringent embargoes on the Press). Clearly democratisation of information is to be welcomed. Nevertheless, society still requires reliability, or 'weight of testimony' in the written word. The poet-seer had a role in Greek history, just as the author does in ours. The trouble with the spread of the written word on the Internet is that it is beginning to look like democracy run wild. There is so much written information out there, that it is difficult to know what to trust.

Trust is based on a respect for authority that is deeply ingrained in both Western and Eastern cultures. It is based on respect for people in positions of strength – strength that, whether or not backed by military might, owes its origins to an individual capacity to keep a finger on the pulse of the times. Those people who achieve public respect are generally asserting the spirit of the age – 'what oft was Thought, but ne'er so well Exprest', as Pope put it.

It is no coincidence that, in Romance languages at least, it is from verbal strength that the term 'authority' acquires its meaning. Its connection with authorship is within the etymology of the language itself: *auctor* 'a person who originates or gives existence to anything' and *auctoritatem* 'title to be believed; weight of testimony'. That weight is further stamped by the publisher's imprint and its reputation.

The challenge facing writers today is to preserve a former role whilst embracing the new opportunities; to ensure that the authority in authorship remains secure. Without print on paper, that is no easy matter: because reading is no longer close and careful study; reading is 'using'. Reading nowadays equals downloading (even though more is downloaded than is ever read). And downloading (without the stick-of-rock watermarking) all too easily crops the authors' names from their texts, rendering their words free for all. Why should we mind this? Isn't it a Utopian view of the world, one in which all knowledge is shared, ideas passed on, embroidered upon, re-issued in new forms? Aren't we just returning to the rhetoric of the oral culture, where 'Homer' doesn't designate one man but a collaboration of shared inventiveness, and all the better for it?

The trouble with the above argument is that while it is no doubt in the spirit of the age to edit and expand on other people's work according to post-modernist principles, we must be able to lodge, somewhere, an authenticated, definitive version of the original work. There must be a traceable reliability chain so that the reader-user knows the brand-name pedigree of the work under scrutiny. It is essential to know whether we are getting, say, a Christian Dior original or the *prét à porter* street version. It is important to know, when reading a medical text, that the decimal points in a dosage chart have not slipped along a few digits by some quirk of technology. And it is important that the writer of a digitally distributed work can be uniquely identified with it for reasons of trust, quality control and – where required – payment.

The world has seen a free-for-all unregulated press: in a brief Jacobin era in France between 1790 and 1792. Defamatory and pornographic material abounded unchecked, the serious press stood still and waited; *droit d'auteur* was born in 1793. Deconstruction didn't work then and it's a reasonable guess that it will not work now.

Censorship

As for censorship – the obverse of democracy – the Internet has moved on a great deal from its early beginnings, when you could find unbridled fascism, violence and pornography with some ease. Now that a few test cases have ruled that Internet Service Providers bear some of the responsibility for making sites available to their customers, there is some censorship to exclude defamatory or offensive material. You can also have it tailor-made by using net-nannying software (mentioned above), by customising some of the access options in your browser, and by choosing an ISP that already filters out certain kinds of content.

English access

Computer-speak will never be as rich a source of vocabulary as war or religion or sport, but it will be interesting to watch developments. Computerese is creeping into metaphor. 'Feel free to visit my website and mouse around,' people say. Even the word 'access', which is an old library word, has new connotations now.

But there's more to access than a shift in word meaning. Access for whom? Although some of the search engines (e.g. AltaVista) offer acceptable mechanical translations of web pages on the fly, English is still the *lingua franca* of the Internet. This is alarming for some nations - the French, for example, fear a diminution of their own influence as the electronic media bind the commercial world together through the operating standards of the English tongue – American English, to be more accurate.

Search engines offer an interesting rough tool for taking a snapshot of the current state of English on the Internet. I tried out a few variants. Hotbot turned up 99,930 matches for the word 'organise' (with an 's'), for example, and 406,530 'organize' (with a 'z'). Or 484,200 for 'colour' and 3,009,050 for 'color'; 1,995,600 for 'centre' and 7,291,040 for 'center'. American spelling rules; not surprisingly, as there have historically been more people using the Internet in the US than anywhere else. There's a shift, though. In the year 2000, non-English languages (combined) on the Net account for more than half of web-page content. English dominance may be on the wane.

Health hazards

It cannot be denied that there are health hazards related to the use of computers, and being on the Internet means using the computer even more. In particular 'mousing around' puts a strain on the wrist and the back of the neck. I know, because I have had Repetitive Strain Injury (RSI) recently – induced, I firmly believe, by too much webbery. I'm supported by a survey by Interface Analysis Associates which finds a greater risk of RSI in surfing the web than carrying out other computer tasks.

Ergonomics

A buzz-word, this, meaning that work should adjust to the body, not you to it. Writers who sit all day can often be very cavalier about their own comfort and well-being. It's not easy to spoil yourself, but it is the best insurance against backache, headaches and debilitating limb diseases. The hundred-odd journalists from *The Financial Times* who were referred for medical treatment were all sitting at desks of the 'wrong' height on uncomfortable chairs and with poor lighting. Office journalists can now rely on their employers to get these things right; freelance journalists have to take care of themselves.

Ailments from backache to serious incapacitation can be prevented by making sure your equipment is comfortably placed and properly lit. The desk should be low enough for your hands to be relaxed, i.e. with the hands in a continuous line with your wrists and forearms and these roughly parallel to the floor. The keyboard should be tiltable and separated from the screen because it is then easier to find a comfortable arm position. You should also have space to rest your arms in front of the keyboard. The monitor should be positioned so its centre is just below eye-level: this may be higher than when it stands on the system unit. If you are typing out a manuscript, try to get a document holder that will enable you to avoid uncomfortable head movements and eye strain.

The chair should be low enough for both feet to be firmly on the floor or on a footrest and should have adjustable back support. If using a knee-rest type of chair, make sure it is adjustable and there is no pressure anywhere (difficult, that).

Lighting is also part of your working-room's health. You're supposed to have a dual lighting arrangement – diffused ceiling lighting to give a low-level all-round light and clear illumination on your working copy. No bulbs in the line of vision, or reflected in the computer screen.

Eye strain

Lacemakers' eye strain has always laid writers low, but the flicker of the screen does exacerbate it. Get a really high-quality screen with clear definition of characters. Look away from the screen from time to time because the eye strain is partially caused by fixed staring which dries out the eyes. Reduce glare, too, by window blinds against the sun and by placing the screen at 90 degrees to the window.

Repetitive Strain Injury

Familiarly known as RSI, this is the disease most likely to affect writers. There are two main types: tenosynovitis and upper limb disorders. Both are conditions which come from over-use or incorrect use of the word-processor and cause acute pain and swelling in the joints of the hands, arms and sometimes the legs. Some writers are so badly affected that they cannot work for months. The disease can take years out of your working life and you may get no warning signs until it incapacitates you. If you do get a slight twinge, or a feeling of tingling or numbness in your hand, don't ignore it.

Writers who compose straight onto the word-processor are at less risk than those who do the first draft by hand and then type it out for revising because composing straight onto the screen is more of a stop and start activity and gives the writer more variation of movement. The real culprits are too much immobility and the seductive nature of writing with a word-processor, which can beguile writers into carrying on just a little bit too long.

If you do get RSI, rest and time are the best cures, though I found acupuncture effective. Passive physiotherapy can help, e.g. rest the hands on the thighs and lift one finger at a time; put your hands together in the prayer position and try to raise the elbows; rest the backs of the hands together and drop the elbows.

ture

..ce are several unanswerable ontological questions dotted through this book. It *is* addressed to writers and so it has writerly concerns at its heart. On the one hand, writers can turn the ease of digital copying to their own advantage in the wide opportunities it presents for research, communication and personal publishing. But at the same time, the proliferation of copying as an ethic means that the 'original' work may cease to have a value in twenty-first-century society. Even if the admiration for an original 'aura' takes time to fade, creative artists are having to struggle to affirm the value of traditional activities in a digital world.

In our anxieties about substantiality and authority are we merely reiterating an old argument about the physicality of art objects or is there something new and different about the present age? Should we be glad that rhetoric is giving way to a new form of oralcy? In what qualities does a work of art inhere? Is it, indeed, relevant to talk about works of art as fixed entities at all? The book, like music, should perhaps be happy in its status as a series of digital cyphers, since the work itself resides in its interpretation.

Writers may ask themselves whether the way we have viewed copyright for the last three hundred years (as a piece of property in the UK, and with *droit d'auteur* fostering a concept of personality in France) is limiting the imagination. Perhaps it is constraining creativity down certain set paths. Perhaps there are other types of work for which notions of copyright would be irrelevant. The landscape-wrapping artist Christo cannot – and would not – sell his wrapped works. He has broken out of convention to produce a totally new art form. Some of the multi-authored patchworks in Part 2:6 **Interactivity and experimental forms,** page 177 suggest that written forms could also find a new dimension. They may even return us to nomadic anonymity, a democracy of sharing. Will this free literature from its stasis, or make it chaotic?

The questions above have exercised greater minds than mine over many decades. I have simply tried to single out the author's place in a world where computers join writing to produce a set of problems that are in a continuous tradition – maintaining the cultural and economic importance of the written word.

The growth of the Internet is astounding – from 213 computers registered on the Internet in 1981 to perhaps 300 million users world-wide 20 years later. People have tried to look forward a few years, foreseeing voice-activated devices, smarter artificial intelligence, computers that don't look like computers and which adapt to people – as opposed to people adapting to them. Something unexpected will always turn up. Just when everyone thinks the current round of Internet problems is settling, there'll be a new breakthrough that changes everything we have thought before.

It is hard to imagine now what the next leap forward will be; it is too early to judge. The Internet will not *replace* what we have, but *add to* it. The profession of writing will survive, with traditional forms alongside others that we can only imagine now. The success of these new forms depends partly on the willingness of creative people to engage with technologies that may seem remote and unforgiving at first glance. They are *just* tools, however, that offer different ways of expressing ideas. Ideas and imagination always come first. And audiences will follow where the marriage of creative minds with new technology pushes forward artistic boundaries. 3D animation, interactive games and stories, broadband broadcasting and virtual reality all offer scope for originality. In the beginning was the word, and in the end there is still the word. Whether it is spoken, filmed, animated or written on digital paper, there is always a place for the writer.

Resources for Chapter 8 in Part 2 and online

INTERNET ADDRESSES

More advanced webs, particularly of orb-weaver spiders, are highly intricate, raised above the ground, and oriented to intercept the paths of flying insects. The spinning itself is a complex process involving the placement and then removal of scaffolding spirals and a combination of sticky and nonsticky strands. In some cases a number of spiders will form a kind of communal web, but spiders in general are not social.

'Spider', Microsoft's *Encarta*, 1994

The resource file in the tint-edged pages lists about 800 hand-picked sites for writers, with very brief descriptions and occasional evaluations. The addresses are at the back of the book for ease of reference. They are arranged in chapter order to match the themes in the book, but set out in a continuous listing so that you can more easily see at a glance what's available. Little square screens are not good at providing an overview.

The book's website

Go to the book's website at http://www.internetwriter.co.uk to click-link from there. Or copy individual sections into personal bookmarks (mindful of the remarks on fair dealing). The online addresses will be verified regularly so that dead links are removed and new ones will go up.

Access to the website resource is intended primarily for those who buy a copy of this book so you will be prompted for a password. The password is *qixotica* – all one word. I know that doesn't stop other people who know about the book getting through – nor do I mind – but since this represents hours and hours of surfing tailored specifically for its readership, A & C Black and I agreed that we would not make it universally available.

Look before you dial

All these sites were live just before publication (late 1999), but Internet addresses change just as any other addresses do. That said, there is a growing realisation amongst people who have constructed genuinely useful resources that redirection URLs should link old addresses to a new one. Generally speaking, the better the resource, the more trouble it will take to ensure that people can find it even with an old address. Some URLs will have the word 'purl' at the beginning. PURL stands for Persistent Uniform Resource Locator and is a clue that the owner of the resource is committed to keeping the site stable and available. A PURL address won't lead you to a dead link and should mean that the same URL will always point to the same resource even if, behind the scenes, it has moved somewhere else.

Interpreting the URL

You can tell quite a lot from the URL itself – it's like reading any other address. Is it Belgravia or Brixton? It's unadventurous to be prejudiced and you can be wrong, but here are a few pointers.

Individuals or establishments who have invested resources in creating web pages that *excel* will have registered short domain names descriptive of their organisations. This is, after all, publishing and a background in design, editing and communications is an advantage. So short and snappy is good; long is a giveaway that it is a subdirectory branching off another site.

A URL with the squiggly sign '~' (called a tilde) is probably someone's personal page on a public or academic server. However, this does not mean that the information is necessarily of poor quality. The same applies to URLs with a series of forward slashes, '/', and a name or number interspersed. If there's a hash character '#' then the reference is taking you to a particular point on a longer page.

It can be very useful to delete part of the right-hand side of the URL to see where the new, shorter URL takes you. Delete from the right-hand side to the slashes to move up the directory tree.

If the URL has 'aol' in it, that stands for America Online and AOL operates in the UK as well as in the US (as does CompuServe); 'edu' is also American. Anything with a '.uk' in it is

British; but you can't always tell with 'com', 'org' or 'net' – they can be both.

Of course, there's some very good content on personal pages, but with so much to choose from, how do you know whom to trust? For example, home pages from the service providers Bigfoot and Geocities can be a very mixed bag. There are some very good ones and some dismally poor.

Most people will go for brand names they know or have reason to feel may be trustworthy. That's what publication is all about. So

Oxford University Press
http://www.oup.co.uk

is bound to be worthy. A long URL like this:

Creative Writing Workshop
http://cyberschool.4j.lane.edu/people/faculty/Hamill/writers/writers.html

may need interpreting. 'edu' tells you it is an educational establishment in the US; 'cyberschool' may have you wondering how academic; 'people/faculty' indicates that the page itself ('writers.html') was written by a member of staff – 'Hamill'. That could alert you to some instability – 'Hamill' may have left the establishment. In fact, the date on the page is 1997 and my email of enquiry received no reply, so it is not in my listings.

In the end, the market will decide how the future will develop. Even the brand names that carry kudos at present will die if publishers fail to re-invent themselves in line with what customers want and the market will take. The market wants easy access. Note: I did not say 'free'. The future is surely about delivering quality information at reasonable and acceptable prices easily, safely and to as wide a range of clients (public and private) as possible.

Checklist of questions

You must be sure in your own mind what you are looking for and why you have come to the site. Otherwise, the chances are you'll sink into unfocused channel-hopping. Once there, you can tell a lot by the look and feel. Poor spelling and grammar abounds: it's usually the sign of a poorly thought-out site (though even the best have typos here and there).

Look for these things:

- a statement of the aims and objectives of the site
- a site map to give an overall picture of what there is to see
- author and publisher details and an email link to back up authenticity
- details of the origin of any data or information
- mention of any quality checks or referencing of the information
- creation dates – age may or may not matter
- last updated dates – shows how active a site is
- clearly marked archival information
- good design and awareness of readability – though many excellent academic papers scrawl in Courier head-to-toe across the screen
- a good search box – vital on an information-rich site

In judging the content, ask yourself:

- Does the resource appear to be honest and genuine?
- Is the resource available in another format? (e.g. a book or CD-ROM)
- Do any of the materials infringe copyright?
- Is the information well researched?
- Is any bias made clear and of an acceptable level?
- Is it the result of a personal hobby-horse?
- Is the information durable in nature?
- Is there adequate maintenance of the information content?

What follows is a set of bookmarks, arranged alphabetically and in the subject order relating to the sections in Part 1. Section 6 is classified by genre – though I couldn't represent every single interest group. If anything is missing, please look at the subject guides in the section on search engines.

Online resources

All resources are online at http://www.internetwriter.co.uk *password = qixotica*

1. Getting connected

New to the web

BBC Web Wise – getting started on the Internet; first-rate site with good mini-essays nicely pitched; all you need (if you can read the tiny print on coloured backgrounds)
http://www.bbc.co.uk/education/webwise

FAQ – Frequently Asked Questions on just about anything to do with the Internet
http://www.faqs.org

New to the Web – a basic tutorial with a good glossary
http://home.netscape.com/netcenter/newnet

NetLearn – non-profit directory of resources for learning and teaching Internet skills, including resources for WWW, email and other formats
http://www.rgu.ac.uk/schools/sim/research/netlearn/callist.htm

What is? – computer and Internet jargon explained
http://whatis.com

Quality Internet Training – provides Internet training throughout the UK and is funded by Joint Information Systems Committee (JISC)
http://www.netskills.ac.uk

Writers' Internet Guide – another site associated with a book; somewhat ad hoc content
http://www.on-writing.com

Internet culture

Acronym Expander – find any web abbreviation or acronym
http://www.ucc.ie/info/net/acronyms

History of the Web
http://www.w3.org/people/Berners-Lee/shorthistory.html

Internet Café Database – all over the world, so useful if you are travelling
http://www.netcafes.com
http://www.netcafeguide.com

Internet Cafés in the UK – find a venue near you to try out going online
http://www.internet-magazine.com/resources/caffs.htm

Internet at Public Libraries in the UK – more and more of these are opening up
http://www.earl.org.uk/access

Web access tools

Association of Shareware Professionals
http://www.asp-shareware.org

Cookie Central – all about the knotty problem of what they are and whether it's a privacy issue
http://www.cookiecentral.com

Shareware – some of the best free and nearly free software; safe to download
http://www.shareware.com

Tucows – silly name acronym for The Ultimate Collection Of Windows Software; good freeware source
http://www.tucows.com

Stuffit – decompression software primarily for Mac but also in a PC version
http://www.aladdinsys.com/expander/index.html

Winzip – decompression software for PC
http://www.winzip.com

The cross-platform page: encoding and compression formats – this is a seriously technical page but for those having difficulty in sharing scripts between Mac and PC, it has all the answers; also good on audio and video formats
http://x3066.resnet.cornell.edu/xplat/xplat.comp.html

Uploading and downloading
FTP Explorer – friendly file transfer software for PC
http://www.ftpx.com

WS_FTP – slightly more technical file transfer software for PC
http://www.csra.net/junodj/ws_ftp.htm

Netfinder – file transfer software for Mac
http://www.ozemail.com.au/~pli/netfinder

Plug-ins
Adobe Acrobat Reader – free from this site and needed for long documents in PDF form
http://www.adobe.com/products/acrobat/readstep.html

LiquidAudio – for downloading copyright-cleared music
http://www.liquidaudio.com/index.html

QuickTime
http://www.apple.com/quicktime

RealAudio
http://www.realaudio.com

Shockwave and Flash
http://www.macromedia.com/software

2. Email

Guidelines and people
Finding people on email
http://www.whowhere.lycos.com/Email

BT PhoneNetUk – online UK telephone directory searchable by personal and business name
http://www.bt.com/phonenetuk

Royal Mail – look up postcodes, postage calculations, stamp collecting and more
http://www.royalmail.co.uk

Anti-spam page
http://spam.abuse.net

Campaign for Unmetered Telecommunications – go there and sign up your support for the campaign if it hasn't succeeded by the time you read this
http://www.unmetered.org.uk

Email Site – with how-to-use tutorials, setting up mailing lists and junk filtering software
http://www.emailtoday.com

Email Guidelines and netiquette – from Oxford University
http://www.oucs.ox.ac.uk/documentation/leaflets/L03.html

Free email voice player – the free player that goes with the Voice Email below so your colleagues can listen to your recorded email
http://www.bonzi.com/freeplay/vemplay.htm

Voice Email – low cost add-on program for Windows that uses the power of human speech to create audio email messages by simply talking; an answer to RSI?
http://www.bonzi.com/voiceemail/voice.asp

Free email and web space
CallNet – first free UK 0800 Internet service; others sure to follow
http://www.callnet.0800.com

Free Email Address Directory
http://www.emailaddresses.com

Top 10 free ISPs – a personal view; full listing too
http://www.h-h-l.co.uk

Yahoo's list of free ISPs
http://www.yahoo.co.uk/Regional/Countries/United_Kingdom/Business_and_Economy/Companies/Internet_Services/Access_Providers/Free_Services

Telco charges compared
http://www.magsy.co.uk/telecom

Homestead – free web space and chat with no programming skills
http://www.homestead.com

i-drive – 25 megabytes of free, secure online disk space to store and access your files from any web browser in the world
http://www.idrive.com

UK2.Net – inexpensive domain registration and web forwarding
http://uk2.net

Webb Net – free web space with wizard to help you set it up; a community-creating site for the arts
http://www.webb.net/webb

Commercial ISPs
Internet Magazine – top listings every month
http://www.internet.magazine.com

Demon
http://www.demon.co.uk

Pipex
http://www.dial.pipex.com

See also JOURNALISM (6)

3. The World Wide Web

Dictionaries and directories
Andy's Anagram Solver
http://www.ssynth.co.uk/~gay/anagram.html

Bartletts Familiar Quotations
http://www.bartleby.com/index.html

Bibliographical Society of London – learned society dealing with the study of the book and its history.
http://speke.ukc.ac.uk/secl/bibsoc/index.html

Bibliomania – excellent full text with a good word or phrase retrieval; includes the wonderful *Brewer's Dictionary of Phrase & Fable* (which no author can do without)
http://www.bibliomania.com

Britannica.com – a new and huge resource of free information, grammar and all reference links; Encyclopaedia Britannica online
http://www.britannica.com

CIA World Factbook – statistical data about countries and other useful data
http://www.gov/cia/publications/factbook

CobuildDirect Information – service for accessing a 56 million-word corpus of modern English language text, written and spoken; subscription necessary
http://titania.cobuild.collins.co.uk/direct_info.html

Encyberpedia – free (and not as good as Britannica)
http://www.encyberpedia.com/ency.htm

English as a Second Language for Americans – amusing US-UK dictionary with list of problem words
http://pages.prodigy.com/NY/NYC/britspk/main.html

EURODICAUTOM online multilingual dictionary
http://www2.echo.lu/edic

KnowEurope – new online resource offering access to a broad range of information about the EU and the wider Europe
http://www.knoweurope.net

KnowUK – provides key information about the people, institutions and organisations of the United Kingdom; *Debrett, Hansard, Who's Who, Who Was Who, Dictionary of Biography* and 30-40 licensed copyright texts. For libraries because of seriously high charge; schools version due
http://www.knowuk.co.uk

NISS – Reference and Bibliographic Services; bibliographic material round the world
http://www.niss.ac.uk/reference/index.html

The Quotations Page – a personal collection plus a quote of the day
http://www.starlingtech.com/quotes

Research-it – little battery of dictionaries and acronym converters
http://www.itools.com/research-it

Roget's Thesaurus – 1911 version (out of copyright, and inevitably out of currency too)
http://humanities.uchicago.edu/forms_unrest/ROGET.html

Virtual Reference Desks – various dictionaries and acronym converters – US-based
http://thorplus.lib.purdue.edu/reference/index.html
http://www.refdesk.com

WISDOM: Knowledge & Literature Search – links to writing and literature sites under the headings Creativity, Literature, Authors, Thoughts, Publishing, Words, Languages
http://thinkers.net

WWWebster Thesauruses – Merriam Webster thesaurus
http://www.m-w.com/thesaurus.htm

Education and teaching writing

See also CRITIQUING AND WRITING WORKSHOPS (4) and ACADEMIC WRITING (6)

BBC – educational information and much else; first class resource in all areas
http://www.bbc.co.uk/education

Common Mechanical Errors in College Writing
http://www.usafa.af.mil/dfeng/errors.htm

Computers in Teaching Initiative – 24 subject-based Centres working to support the use of communication and information technologies in UK higher education
http://www.cti.ac.uk

DeVry's Online Writing Support Center – for writing students
http://www.devry-phx.edu

English Composition 'Comp' site – thoughtful educational site for teaching skills and exploring issues
http://www.abacon.com/compsite

English Through the Internet – reading and writing skills
http://www.tcom.ohiou.edu/OU_Language/english/writing.html

Essay Writing for Students – to encourage consistency, clarity and precision in written and published work
http://www.pol.adfa.oz.au/resources/essay_writing/contents.html

Glossary of Rhetorical Terms – linked list of all the major schemes from classical and medieval rhetoric
http://www.uky.edu/ArtsSciences/Classics/Harris/rhetform.html

How We Write – a book site for a book on the psychology of writing
http://www.routledge.com/routledge/rcenters/linguistics/sharp.html

Online Resource For Writers – advice on writing, research, punctuation, et al.
http://www.ume.maine.edu/~wcenter/resource.html

Pen & Sword Hypersite – American society contemplating itself interactively
http://www.rahul.net/jag

Resources for Teachers of Writing – writing across the curriculum, writing in the disciplines
http://www.english.uiuc.edu/cws/wworkshop/ww_wac.html#tools

Rhetoric and Composition
http://english–www.hss.cmu.edu/rhetoric

Study Web – school research aid sorted by topic including one on writers and writing
http://www.studyweb.com

Teaching Writing – links to resources on pedagogy of writing; various writing genres
http://www.smpcollege.com

Tutor2000 – online tutor referral service helping tutors and students find each other over the Internet
http://www.tutor2000.com

Write Environment Inc. – website for teachers of writing; may give ideas
http://www.writeenvironment.com

Writing & Computers Association – research into the effect of technology on writing
http://ibs.derby.ac.uk/~markt/WC11/WC_info.html

Evaluating sources

Evaluating Information Found on the Internet
http://milton.mse.jhu.edu/research/education/net.html
Evaluating Internet Research Sources
http://www.sccu.edu/faculty/R_Harris/evalu8it.htm

Evaluating Web Resources
http://www.science.widener.edu/~withers/webeval.htm

How to Evaluate a Web Page
http://manta.library.colostate.edu/howto/evalweb.html

Information overload
Reuters business report
http://www.reuters.com/rbb/research/overloadframe.htm
an (undated) dissertation by student at Queen Margaret University College, Edinburgh
http://www.geocities.com/Tokyo/Subway/7854/abs.htm

Thinking Critically about World Wide Web Resources
http://www.library.ucla.edu/libraries/college/instruct/web/critical.htm

Libraries

See also SECTION 6

Ask a Librarian – national reference enquiry service for the public provided by public libraries throughout the UK
http://www.earl.org.uk/ask/index.html

Bodleian Library
http://www.rsl.ox.ac.uk/welcome.html

BookWhere 2000 – software that searches hundreds of library catalogues and databases of published information on the Internet. Evaluation version available; aimed at institutions
http://www.bookwhere.com

British Library – free search for material held in the major Reference and Document Supply collections of the British Library
http://portico.bl.uk

British Library's Document Supply Centre – for research and private study in compliance with UK copyright law
http://www.bl.uk/services/bsds/dsc/delivery.html

Catalogues, national biographies, indexes to periodical contents, and a list of all online services provided by the European national libraries, Glasgow University Library
http://www.gla.ac.uk/Library/E-Journals/index.html

Central Office of Information
http://www.coi.gov.uk/coi

On-demand publishing in Higher Education – a national database and resource bank of electronic texts; copyright licences
http://www.stir.ac.uk/infoserv/heron/project.htm

INFOTRIEVE – library services company offering full-service document delivery, databases on the web, and ways of identifying, retrieving and paying for published literature
http://www.infotrieve.com

Internet Public Library – reference section containing subject overviews, biography, etc.
http://www.ipl.org

Library and Related Resources – comprehensive Library materials at Exeter University
http://www.ex.ac.uk/~ijtilsed/lib/wwwlibs.html

Library of Congress – digital library collections and services
http://lcweb.loc.gov/homepage/lchp.html

Library Link – online information and discussion forum for Librarians and Information Professionals
http://www.mcb.co.uk/liblink

Stumpers – archives of an email-based resource for reference librarians to help each other find the answers to difficult questions; good to browse
http://www.cuis.edu/~stumpers

Statistics links
http://www.ons.gov.uk/links/links.htm

University Research Libraries
http://www.leeds.ac.uk/library/general/curluse.htm
http://copac.ac.uk/copac

Reference miscellany

Eponym – aimed at new parents and handy if you are looking for a suitable name for a character; names from just about everywhere in the world at different time periods
http://student-www.uchicago.edu/~smhawkin/names

Famous Birthdays – month-by-month and day-by-day listing of birth dates, historial and in the media
http://www.famousbirthdays.com

Famous Firsts – people who did something first arranged in ascending date order
http://m2.aol.com/JuliannaA/1-triv.html

Dying Words – for the historical novelist
http://members.aol.com/WordPlays/dying.html

Internet Resources Newsletter
http://www.hw.ac.uk/libWWW/irn/irn.html

Literary Calendar: An Almanac of Literary Information – significant literary events: births, deaths, publications
http://litcal.yasuda-u.ac.jp/LitCalendar.shtml

Metric/imperial conversion – Celsius to Fahrenheit; metres in a mile; and others
http://www.frenchproperty.com/ref/convert.htm

Perpetual Virtual Calendars – a historical or science fiction novelist's dream: verify any date or day of the week in the 20th and 21st centuries
http://www.mnsinc.com/utopia/Calendar/Virtual_Calendars.html

References for Writers
http://www.humberc.on.ca/~coleman/cw-ref.html

Time Zone Converter – what time it is or will be any time in the world
http://www.timezoneconverter.com

Today in History – US-based; e.g. did not have Shakespeare's birthday or St George's day on 23 April when searched
http://lcweb2.loc.gov/ammem/today/today.html

Who is or Was – good for checking people's dates; incorporates the Cambridge Dictionary of American Biography which maybe boosts the US content, but not too much
http://www.biography.com

Word Museum – not what you might think it is; interviews, articles and author pages
http://www.wordmuseum.com

The Writer's Almanac – daily snippets of poetry and history from a broadcast hosted by Garrison Keillor
http://almanac.mpr.org

Texts online
See also ELECTRONIC ORIGINATION (5)

Bible Gateway
http://bible.gospelcom.net/bible

Classics – links to the full text of 400 Greek and Roman classics in translation.
http://the-tech.mit.edu/Classics/titles.d.html

Electronic Text Center – collection of online English-language texts; links to other texts online by subject or by author
http://etext.lib.virginia.edu/english.html

The English Server – large collection of interesting resources
http://english-server.hss.cmu.edu

Etext Archives – archives of religious, political, legal and fanzine text
http://www.etext.org

Literature Online – poetry, literature and reference databases aimed at libraries because of high charge, but you can try it free; also some free access to poetry and to a writer in residence
http://lion.chadwyck.co.uk

Oxford Text Archive – distributes more than 2500 resources in over 25 different languages for study purposes only
http://www.hcu.ox.ac.uk/ota/public/index.shtml

Project Gutenberg – the official sites (many mirrors all over the world); vast library of e-texts, mostly public domain; all in plain text format
http://www.gutenberg.net

Shakespeare Resources – links to quantities of others
http://www

Search engines
AltaVista – has always been solid; has an interesting and quite useful translation feature
http://altavista.digital.com

Excite – good at text searching, friendly for beginners, good people finding
http://www.excite.com

Google – useful for the sciences
http://www.google.com

HotBot – friendly and pretty comprehensive
http://www.hotbot.com

Interactive portal for the UK with news, weather, maps
http://www.2b.co.uk

Lycos – first popular engine, but now slipping back; less good at complex searching, nice coverage of communities
http://www.lycos.co.uk

Magellan – more like an online guide; strength is in the quality of its subject reviews
http://www.mckinley.com

Northern Light – fast and accurate and said to index more pages than any other engine; good on reviews, books, magazines and news wires
http://www.northernlight.com

Search Engine Watch
http://www.searchenginewatch.com

Search UK – UK-only material; not a favourite
http://www.searchuk.co.uk

Webcrawler – useful subject channels
http://Webcrawler.com

Yahoo! – not so good on text searching as others but good subject sorting
http://www.yahoo.co.uk

Multi-search portals
All-One-Search – 500 search engines, databases, indexes and directories in a single site; plus price comparisons on books; impressively comprehensive and worth looking at if only to find the engine that specialises in something esoteric
http://www.allonesearch.com

AskJeeves – only has selected sites picked by real editors and searches across AltaVista, Excite, Infoseek, Webcrawler and Yahoo!; a good starting point
http://www.askjeeves.com

Classical Search – global search engine for the classical music Internet community; more than 15,000 international classical music sites; useful for music journalists
http://www.classicalsearch.com

Dogpile – terrible name, but it's good, especially for single word searches
http://dogpile.com

Inference Find – parallel searching with grouped results
http://www.inference.com/infind

Information Please Almanac – busy interface; good on current events
http://www.infopls.com

Infoseek Express – portal for many of the other search engines listed; available for download and personalising
http://express.infoseek.com

Metacrawler – parallel searches of seven major search engines; popular sites mainly
http://www.metacrawler.com

SearchIQ – tells users which search engine to try for their particular needs; also suggests a successful 3-phase strategy; a good starting point
http://www.searchiq.com

WebFerret – powerful downloadable software (free evaluation) for maxi-searching across engines; customisable versions
http://www.ferretsoft.com/netferret

Intelligent agents
Bullseye – intelligent searching software across 450 or so engines; free evaluation
http://www.oxford-knowledge.co.uk/bullseye.htm

Discovery Agent – web-based alerting service that delivers customised information; subscribers create, manage and edit their own personal profiles
http://www.isinet.com/products/ias/da.html

Mind-it – billed as having your own research assistant track any topic you want

and alert you as soon as it changes
http://www.netmind.com/html/url-minder.html

My Yahoo!
http://my.yahoo.com

PointCast Network – personal agent providing customised news, continually updated
http://www.pointcast.com

POOL – personalised search agent that says it learns your preferences
http://netbeta.sogang.ac.kr/~kmin

Webcatcher
http://www.dev-com.com/~rfactory/webcatcher.html

Subject guides
Britannica Internet Guide – good coverage in science, arts, history and geography
http://www.ebig.com

E-book-based search portal
http://www.ebookcity.com

Info Service – news and information focus
http://info-s.com

NetGuide – technology network
http://www.netguide.com

Open Text – UK business resource
http://index.opentext.net

Subject-based gateways – clearing houses to quality assessed Internet resources
http://www.lub.lu.se/desire/sbigs.html

When to use AND and NOT – Boolean logic explained
http://www.cnet.com/Resources/Tech/Advisers/Search/search3.html

Viruses and hoaxes
Anti-virus software database – good starting point leading to other links
http://www.hitchhikers.net/antivirus/antivirus-dis.phtml

Dr Solomon's Virus Central – full information about viruses
http://www.drsolomon.com/vircen/index.cfm

Identifying hoaxes
http://www.philb.com/hoaxes.htm

Viruses, myths and urban legends
http://kumite.com/myths

4. Virtual communities
The Virtual Community – Howard Rheingold's book online
http://www.rheingold.com

The Well – one of the very first free online communities, now charges $10 a month
http://www.well.com

Newsletters
E-zine for Writers in the new Millennium
http://www.fictionhouse.com

Inklings – newsletter for writers on the Net
http://www.inkspot.com/inklings

The Internet Writing Journal
http://www.writerswrite.com/journal

Speculations – magazines for writers who want to be read
http://www.speculations.com

Writer's Block – an e-zine with lots of articles on writing generally
http://www.niva.com/writblok/index.htm

Writer Online – e-zine; also has writers' software resources
http://www.novalearn.com/sites/ink.htm

Writing Now – monthly e-zine dedicated to helping writers market their works to traditional and emerging media
http://www.writingnow.com

Critiquing and writing workshops
Better Writing – free 3-week course sent by email
http://www.freetown.comTheWaterFront/MermaidBeach/1069/index.html

E-Writers
http://e-writers,net

FictionWriter's Connection – provides help with novel writing and information on finding agents and editors and getting published; has mailing list of 3000+
http://www.fictionwriters,com

For writers – self-help; links and professional markets
http://www.forwriters.com

4-Writers – free online fiction courses (six lessons) are offered six times a year
http://4-writers.com

Freelance Success – detailed US-based market information; has good general advice on getting published by top magazines
http://www.freelancesuccess.com

Internet Writing Workshop – six genre-relating mailing lists
listserv@psuvm.psu.edu subscribe writing

Misc.writing – a miscellany about writing
http://www.scalar.com/mw

Online handbook for writers – produced by the University of Victoria
http://www.clearcf.uvic.ca/writersguide/Pages/MasterToc.html

Online writing community
http://trace.htu.ac.uk

Word Weave – writing tips, including character creation tutorial for beginner writers
http://www.geocities.com/Wellesley/Veranda/2932/wordweav/index.html

WRITE and REWRITE
http://www.writelinks.com

W.R.I.T.E. HomePage
http://www.cstudies.ubc.ca/write/write.html

Writers
http://www.bocklabs.wisc.edu/ims/writers.html

Writer's Block
http://web.mit.edu/mbarker/www/writers/technical.html#Writer'sBlock

Writer's Block – an e-zine with lots of articles on writing generally; also tips on block
http://www.niva.com/writblok/index.htm

Writers' Circles – has directory of 600 circles in the UK
http://www.cix.co.uk/~oldacre

Writers' Circles in the UK
http://www.author.co.uk/circles.html

Writers' Club University – fee-based classes
http://www.writersclub.com/wcu/catalog.cfm

Writer's Digest – US markets and fiction writing tutorials
http://www.writersdigest.com

Writer's Guidelines Database – excellent resource for the US market; if only there were a UK one too
http://mav.net/guidelines

Writers Net – Internet directory of published writers; includes discussion groups and a directory of literary agents who do not charge reading fees
http://www.writers.net

Writers on the Net
http://www.writers.com

Writers and the Online World – tuition offered
http://www.aaaim.com/laurab/index.htm

Writer's Website Discussion Board
http://www.writerswebsite.com/ww/bbs

Writer's Workshop
http://www.digiserve.com/connect/writers/writhome.shtml

The Writery Cafe
http://.missouri.edu/~writery/cafe.html

The Writing Centre – long and short courses and a scheme called the 'Fiction Writer's Colleague'
http://www.tta-press.freewire.co.uk/writing-centre. html

The Writing Workshop
http://www.geocities.com/~lkraus/workshop/index.html

UK Authors online – an opportunity to publish and link to anglophiliac website
http://www.britishliterature.com

UK Yellow Web: Advice for Writers
http://www.yell.co.uk/ukyw/directory/advwriters/index.html

Writing courses
(non online venues)

International Summer Courses Centre for Continuing Education (University of Edinburgh)
http://www.cce.ed.ac.uk

Knuston Hall
http://www.knustonhall.org.uk

Missenden Abbey
http://www.aredu.demon.co.uk/
missendenabbey

Mailing lists

Easy
Acceptable use policy – applies to all mailing lists
http://www.mailbase.ac.uk/docs.aup.html

Dejanews – archives of news and good access to useful groups
http://www.dejanews.com

Liszt – a search engine for mailing lists
http://www.liszt.com

Free mailing lists from:
http://www.listbot.com
http://www.onelist.com

Publicly Accessible Mailing Lists – thousands of specialist email discussion groups
http://www.neosoft.com/internet/paml

Writer's Workshop Webring – set up or join a writers' ring in any genre
http://romance-central.com/Workshops/
ring.htm

Advanced
Listserv – how to set up and manage Internet mailing lists
http://www.lsoft.com

Majordomo – how to set up and manage Internet mailing lists (requires an understanding of perl scripting)
http://www.greatcircle.com/majordomo

Chat
The Hitchhiker's Guide To The Galaxy – a reference-cum-chat work consisting of hundreds of entries on subjects ranging from aerosol deodorants to zoos
http://www.h2g2.com

Cybercity – regular poetry readings
http://www.blaxxun.com

Cybertown
http://www.cybertown.com

Delphi Forums – pioneer chat and forum venue; free chat rooms and web page
http://forums.delphi.com

Direct link to getting your own chat room
http://www.delphi.com/dir-app/service/
partner.asp

Webb Me – community chat venue; free home page and associated chat room
http://www.webb.net

Video-conferencing – two of the best
http://www.cuseemeworld.com
http://www.microsoft.com/windows/
netmeeting

5. Electronic imprints

Electronic origination

Submission sites
Sites to submit work to – or buy from

1stBooks Library – e-book distributor (music, films and software too); offers books in PDF format; a 40% deal to established authors; motley collection of stuff – Aesop's Fables is free; others sell for around $5
http://www.1stbooks.com

Authors Direct – a self-publishing show-case linking to UK authors' websites; con-nects to word wizard club
http://www.marleys.com

Bibliobytes – books on computer with author submission advice (New Jersey)
http://www.bb.com

Books on Line – public domain titles as well as opportunities to offer your own work
http://www.books-on-line.com

DLSIJ Press – fiction and non-fiction works by women authors; sensible submis-sion arrangments; 45/55 royalty split
http://dlsijpress.com

Domhan – (American and Irish) for self-publishing
http://www.domhanbooks.com

eBooks.com – Internet Digital Bookstore open February 2000; invites authors to let publisher or agent know about it
http://www.ebooks.com

Fiction Works – about e-books and audio book opportunities
http://www.fictionworks.com

Manuscript Depot – for getting your work to literary agents and publishers (based in Canada)
http://www.manuscriptdepot.com

MesaView – e-book publishing services for writers; they take 15% of sales; finders fees offered for recommendations
http://www.mesaview.com

New Concepts Publishing – specialises in romance writers seeking publication; inexpensive for buyers; not obvious what the advantages to sellers are
http://www.newconceptspublishing.com

Novelon Virtual Library – web-based reading with its own downloadable eBookWorm reader which allegedly prevents plagiarism so offering the self-publisher some safety guarantees; the free books look as if they come from Project Gutenberg
https://www.novelon.com

Online Originals – one of several venues for new writers wanting to get published; a colleague who tried it gave this one the thumbs down, however
http://www.onlineoriginals.com

Previewbooks – a Canadian venture, offers half the book free and then charges $10 for the rest
http://www.previewbooks.com

Rocket Library
http://www.rocket-library.com

Stone Garden Publishing – looking for authors
http://medusa.simplenet.com

Storyteller UK
http://www.storyteller.org.uk

VirtuaBooks – acronym spells The VIRTUE of new AUTHORS writing great BOOKS and is a venue for publishing (and buying) new work in Acrobat format to read on laptops and palmtops
http://virtuabooks.com

Word Archive – New Zealand-based venture offering freelance authors (scientific researchers, news journalists, historians, teachers, scriptwriters) a controlled repository for their work, with royalty-style revenues generated from advertising; alpha-testing when this book went to press
http://www.wordarchive.com

Zoetrope Stories – you submit and critique other stories in exchange; seemingly no remuneration
http://www.zoetrope-stories.com

General
Association of Electronic Publishers
http://members.tripod.com/~BestBooksCom/AEP/aepmembers.html

ClearType – follow this site for latest developments in type readability
http://www.microsoft.com/typography/cleartype

El.pub – high-level news and resources on interactive electronic publishing; EU regulations, etc.
http://www.pira.co.uk/IE

E-Ink Corporation – click-link to see animation of how it works
http://www.eink.com

E-paper
http://www.parc.xerox.com/dhl/projects/epaper

Internet Free Press – resources for publishing e-books and e-journals
http://www.free-press.com

e-books and e-readers
eBookNet – latest information on hardware, software and content for hand-held electronic books
http://www.ebooknet.com/index.htm

Electronic Book Exchange – a working party developing copyright protection and distribution specification
http://www.ebxwg.com

Everybook Inc – electronic tablet aimed at professional and student market with mass market version due late 2000
http://www.everybook.net

Franklin Bookman – pioneer product; now specialises in bibles and language dictionaries
http://www.franklin.com/estore

Glassbook – hardware with parallel software for cross-platform standardisation
http://www.glassbook.com

MIT research – the Handy 21 and other technologies for a pie-in-the-sky future
http://www.lcs.mit.edu/

Mystery e-books to download
http://members.tripod.com/mysterybooks/index.html

netLibrary – free and purchasable titles using the Knowledge Station
http://www.netlibrary.com

Open eBook initiative – format specifications, sponsored by the National Institute of Standards and Technology
http://www.openebook.org

Qubit – a hand-held wireless Internet browser
http://www.qubit.net

Rocket eBook – a portable device that allows you to download books and magazines
http://www.rocket-ebook.com

Softbook – leather bound volume looka-like
https://www.softbook.com

Windows viewer
http://superwin.com/fsupervr.htm

Xlibris reading machine – experimental site to see how technology affects reading
http://www.fxpal.xerox.com/xlibris/

$100,000 annual prize for best e-book original. Search the Microsoft site for details.
http://www.microsoft.com

e-zines
See also ACADEMIC WRITING (6) for electronic journals

Inscriptions – weekly e-zine for professional writers
http://come.to/Inscriptions

Journals of the Week – free access each week to two online full text current and past journal volumes; subscriptions then available
http://www.mcb.co.uk/jotw

The Magazine Rack – the Internet's directory to free online magazines
http://www.magazine-rack.com

Virtual Ink – pointers to e-zine collections of varying quality
http://www.pictograph.com/virtualinkIndices.html

Word – online magazine that pays contributors; rather busy visually, will not appeal to traditionalists
http://www.word.com

Literary and book-related magazines
The Bookseller
http://www.thebookseller.com

Critical Quarterly
http://www.blackwellpublishers.co.uk

Poetry Review
http://www.poetrysoc.com

Publishing News
http://www.publishingnews.co.uk

Scottish Book Collector
http://www.scotbooksmag.demon.co.uk

Songwriting and Composing
http://www.icn.co.uk/gisc.html

The Woman Journalist
http://www.author.co.uk/swwj.html

Young Writer
http://www.mystworld.com/youngwriter

Editing

Copyediting Guidelines
http://www.impressions.com/resources_pgs/
edit_pgs/copyguide.html

Editor.net – my own editorial and writing
services
http://www.editor.net

Electronic Editors – excellent site for
editors
http://www.ikingston.demon.co.uk/ee

Electronic Publishing Discussion Forum
http://www.free-press.com

European Federation of Freelance Writers
http://www.eurofed.org

THE SLOT: A Spot for Copy Editors
http://www.theslot.com

Society of Freelance Editors and Proof-
readers
http://www.sfep.org.uk

Vocabula – impressive-looking editorial
services and writing services to business,
publishers, packagers, etc. US-based
http://www.vocabula.com

Writers@Work – jump site to electronic
bulletin boards where publishers, editors
and media moguls post job announcements of interest to freelancers
http://www.geteducated.com/wgir_ch3.htm

Citation formats
MLA
http://www.mla.org/main_stl.htm
Standards for referencing online documents
http://www.beadsland.com/weapas

Indexing
Cindex
http://www.indexres.com/cindex.html

Macrex indexing program – includes links
to other indexing sites
http://www.cix.co.uk/~hcalvert

Society of Indexers
http://www.socind.demon.co.uk

index-l – internet discussion group for
indexers
listserv@bingvmb.cc.binghamton.edu

Index Research
http://www.indexres.com

English and grammar

A.Word.A.Day – service for word-lovers
mailing out a vocabulary word and its definition to the subscribers every day
http://www.wordsmith.org/awad/index.html

Britannica.com – a new and huge resource
of free information, grammar and all reference links
http://www.britannica.com

Cliché Finder
http://www.westegg.com/cliche

An Elementary Grammar
http://www.hiway.co.uk/~ei/intro.html

English Grammar Clinic
http://www.edunet.com/english/clinic-h.html

Gender-Neutral Pronouns FAQ – who's
using 'sie, hir', 'zie, zir', 'e or ey, eir, em',
etc.
http://www.lumina.net/gnp

Good and Bad English – lots of UK links
to institutions and publishers
http://www.nobunaga.demon.co.uk/htm/
english.htm

Grammar notes by Jack Lynch
http://www.english.upenn.edu/~jlynch/
grammar.html

History of the English Language
http://ebbs.english.vt.edu/hel/hel.html

The King's English – Fowler in the 1908
edition; nicely hyperlinked
http://www.columbia.edu/acis/bartleby/fowler

Online English Grammar
http://www.edunet.com/english/grammar/
index.html

Oxford English Dictionary – has a word of
the day, but you have to go and get it
http://www.oed.com

Thesaurus link page
http://www.willpower.demon.co.uk/thessoft.
htm

Word Puzzles online
http://www.m-w.com/game

Word Wizard Club – news and information about words and writing, word or phrase origins, a selection of coinages, quotes and insults
http://www.wordwizard.com

World Wide Words – cornucopia for anyone interested in words
http://www.quinion.com/words

6. New writing opportunities

Academic writing

See also TEXTS ONLINE (3)

Academic Press Journals – listed alphabetically and by subject; free access to tables of contents and abstracts
http://www.apnet.com/www/journal/journals.htm

ChemWeb – library of chemical journals online – subscription with free access
http://chemweb.com

Clic Here – electronic journal licensing, searchable databases; content is chargeable
http://www.blackwell.co.uk

Discussion list about the production and publication of electronic journals
http://www.ioppublishing.com/Journals

EJournal – all-electronic, email delivered, peer-reviewed, academic periodical; focusses on theory and practice surrounding the creation, transmission, storage, interpretation, alteration and replication of electronic text
http://www.hanover.edu/philos/ejournal

Endocrine Society Electronic Journal
http://www.edoc.com/vjwalkthrough

Information Service – links to information about over 200 journals, many of which are available online
http://www.bubl.ac.uk

Ingenta – collection of academic journals in multi-academic disciplines; free access to contents pages and abstracts
http://www.ingenta.com

ISI – database publisher for scholarly research information in the sciences, social sciences, and arts & humanities
http://www.isinet.com

Jobs for the Academic Community – includes teaching writing too
http://www.jobs.ac.uk

Journal and virtual library
http://www.gold.ac.uk/history/hyperjournal/contents.html

Journals Online News
http://toltec.lib.utk.edu/~jon

Keeping your research up to date – Current Awareness Services
http://www.lboro.ac.uk/library/aware/index.html

The Literati Club – for those who write and edit for journals published by MCB Press; also useful advice on getting work accepted for publication
http://www.mcb.co.uk/literati/nethome.htm

Multimedia, Education and Narrative Organisation
http://meno.open.ac.uk/meno

Online Databases and subject gateways – A-Z listing of all UK journals resources, paying and non-paying
http://www.bath.ac.uk/Library/info/databases/a-z.html

Oxford University Press contents and abstracts of scholarly journals
http://www.oup.co.uk/jnls/list

PeerNet – Electronic peer review; provides a pool of people who are qualified to referee papers (UK-based)
http://www.peer-net.com

Social Science Information Gateway – links to more than 50,000 web pages
http://www.sosig.ac.uk

UnCover abstracts
http://uncweb.carl.org

University of Bath (UK) information service on electronic journals and texts; links to searchable catalogues; electronic journals and papers
http://www.bath.ac.uk/Library/info

University of Loughborough – e-journals service
http://www-server.lboro.ac.uk/library/ejournals.html

Writing Development in Higher Education
http://www.le.ac.uk/tlu/writing-dev-99.html

Business writing

The Biz – UK Business Directory with databases of on and off-line company listings; companies and information online only; supported by advertising
http://www.thebiz.co.uk

Business Information Sources on the Internet – annotated collection of links from the University of Strathclyde Department of Information Science
http://www.dis.strath.ac.uk/business/index.html

Business Intelligence links – access to government selected sites
http://www.earl.org.uk/earlweb/busns.html

Economist Intelligence Unit Online Store – one-stop-shop for international business intelligence
http://store.eiu.com

The Economist – selected material available free. Subscription required for access to the complete weekly web edition of the magazine
http://www.economist.com/index.html

InfoNation – database that allows you to view and compare statistical data for the Member States of the United Nations. Could be useful on occasion, though check dates of material
http://www.un.org/Pubs/CyberSchoolBus/infonation/e_infonation.htm

The Nutshell – business information and information management free searching
http://www.thenutshell.co.uk

Plain English Campaign – to stamp out all forms of gobbledygook, legalese, small print and bureaucratic language
http://www.plainenglish.co.uk

Various commerce links, business in- formation and facts for business writers
http://www.commerce.net
http://ganges.cs.tcd.ie/mepeirce/project.html
http://www.mecklerweb.com

Children

The Children's Book Centre
http://www.childrensbookcentre.co.uk

The Children's Literature Web Guide – lots of working links (but dated 1998)
http://www.acs.ucalgary.ca/~dkbrown/index.html

Children's Writing Resource Center
http://www.mindspring.com/~cbi

The Children's Writing Resource Center – for those who want to write for children
http://www.write4kids.com

Fabula – interactive children's storybooks to promote bilingual literacy
http://www.fabula-eu.org/index.html

Myths and Legends – US based listing with world-wide links
http://pubpages.unh.edu/~cbsiren/myth.html

OK UK Books – children's books in the UK
http://www.okukbooks.com
Puffin Books
http://www.puffin.co.uk

Crime writing & mystery

Alfred Hitchcock – biography and filmography of Hitchcock as well as some of his quotes and essays
http://nextdch.mty.itesm.mx/~plopezg/Kaplan/Hitchcock.html

Crime Writers of Canada
http://www.swifty.com/cwc/cwchome.htm

History of the Mystery site – from Poe to present day
http://www.mysterynet.com/history/mystery

Horror Writers Association
http://www.horror.org

Internet Crimewriting Network – articles of interest to crime writers
http://crimewriters.com/Crime

Investigative Research site – database of 130,000 names in topics such as organised crime, white collar crime, corruption, fraud, finance, politics and banking
http://world.std.com./~mmoore

Murderous Intent Homepage – competitions for mystery writers, writers' guidelines, sample fiction
http://www.teleport.com/~madison

Mysteries Com – a mystery of the day and a database of 10,000 others
http://www.mystery.com

Mysterious Events – lists conferences and events for mystery writers
http://www.slip.net/~cluelass/Events.html

Mystery Connection
http://emporium.turnpike.net/~mystery

Mystery Magazines, Fanzines and Newsletters
http://www.db.dk/dbaa/jbs/tsguide.htm

Mystery Reader's Corner – mysteries in Victorian England
http://www.teleport.com/~alecwest/mystery.htm

The Painted Rock
http://www.paintedrock.com
The Baker Street Connection
http://www.citsoft.com/holmes.html

The Case – weekly stories
http://www.thecase.com

The Magnifying Glass – monthly newsletter
http://emporium.turnpike.net/~mystery/tmg.html

The Poisoned Pen – mystery bookstore plus Criminal Calendar and reference materials
http://www.poisonedpen.com

Unsolved Mysteries Television Show homepage – source of ideas for the mystery writer
http://www.unsolved.com/home.html

Fantasy
See SCIENCE FICTION, FANTASY AND HORROR

Fiction
See INTERACTIVITY AND EXPERIMENTAL FORMS and WRITING TOOLS

Health writers
See STM

Historical research
History – The 18th Century
http://history1700s.about.com

History – The 19th Century
http://history1800s.about.com

History – The 20th Century
http://history1900s.about.com

The 18th century webring – some suspect spelling; some look useful
http://www.jaffebros.com/lee/18th

Bodleian Library Map Room
http://www.bodley.ox.ac.uk/boris/guides/maps

Ryhiner map collection – one of the most valuable and outstanding collections of the world. It consists of more than 15,000 maps, charts, plans and views from the 16th to the 18th century
http://biblio.unibe.ch/stub/ryhiner

A digital library of 18th and 19th century journals
http://www.rsl.ox.ac.uk/ilej

Horror
See SCIENCE FICTION, FANTASY AND HORROR

Interactivity and experimental forms
See also POETRY

'As We May Think' by Vannevar Bush – seminal essay by the supposed father of hypertext originally published in the July 1945 issue of *The Atlantic Monthly*
http://www.ps.unisb.de/~duchier/pub/vbush/vbush.shtml

Alice – a 3D Interactive Virtual Environment; computer simulation program that immerses users in an alternative reality;

this is an interesting (and rather technical) site for the serious virtual reality writer
http://www.cs.virginia.edu/~alice

Alt-X online publishing network – 'where the digerati meet the literati'
http://www.altx.com

Dark Lethe collaborative hyper-novel; illustrates difficulties of multi-patchwork approach
http://www.innotts.co.uk/~leo

Eastgate – new hypertext technologies; publication of serious hypertext, fiction and non-fiction: serious, interactive writing
http://www.eastgate.com

Experiment in hypertext fiction
http://dspace.dial.pipex.com/h.whitehead/hyper.htm

Grammatron – hypertext experimentation site
http://www.grammatron.com

Hyperizons: the Search for Hypertext Fiction
http://www.duke.edu/~mshumate/hyperfic.html

Interactive Fiction Now Magazine
http://www.if-now.demon.co.uk

Interactive Novel Writing – opportunity to add chapters to a moderated collaboration
http://members.aol.com/brenndasue/index.html

Interactive Publishing Alert
http://www.netcreations.com/ipa

InterNovel Home Page – experimental site; exercises in composition, creative writing and screenplay adaptation
http://www.internovel.com/~novel

justin.org – online interactive daily diary; author flourishes from lecture tours based on it
http://www.links.net

Libyrinth – experimental writers who are related by the pair of themes
http://rpg.net/quail/libyrinth

Lies – a short story in which the reader chooses between truth and lies; outcome remains the same
http://www.users.interport.net/~rick/lies/lies.html

Plexus – interface to a flux of ideas contained in the writings and visual works of several artists and writers; worth visiting
http://www.plexus.org

Polynoise – views on the future of the creative world
http://net22.com/qazingulaza/polynoises/frames.html

Postmodern Theory, Culture Studies and Hypertext
http://www.marist.edu/humanities/english/eculture.html

Pyramids of Mars – claims to be first downloadable digital graphic novel
http://www.pyramidsofmars.com

Thresholds – all sorts of electronic art but most incorporates words
http://arts.ucsb.edu/eat/projects

Tim Berners-Lee: Style Guide for Online Hypertext – this is an antique (1992 with some updates) but historically interesting
http://www.w3.org/Provider/Style/Overview.html

TrAce Online Writing Community – Arts Council-funded experimental fiction and poetry site
http://trace.ntu.ac.uk

unHoly island – collaborative project set up as part of a Writing-in-Residency by Alan McDonald
http://www.poptel.org.uk/unholy

Virtual Reality site – 1997 essay on how to tell a story in 3-D space
http://www.vrmlsite.com/apr97/a.cgi/spot1.html

What Is Good Hypertext Writing? – pointers on handling links and an appendix of words to avoid – not maintained, but good advice
http://kbs.cs.tu-berlin.de/~jutta/ht/writing.html

Word Circuits – interesting fiction and poetry site with lots of other links
http://www.wordcircuits.com

Residencies

Writer in Residence – Literature Online has opportunities for poets and others
http://lion.chadwyck.com/about.htm

Writer in Residence – University of Dundee; collaborative projects
http://www.dundee.ac.uk/english/dundpoe1.htm

Writer in Residence – for Continuing Education at the University of Cambridge
http://www.rationalman.demon.co.uk

Journalism

ADAM – Art, Design, Architecture and Media information gateway
http://www.adam.ac.uk

AHDS – Arts and Humanities Data Service
http://ahds.ac.uk

The American Prospect – liberal philosophy, politics and public life; some very good articles cutting across cultural boundaries
http://epn.org/prospect.html

American Society of Journalists and Authors – active and supportive union
http://www.asja.org

ByLine – an electronic syndication service for journalists associated with the Authors' Licensing and Collecting Society
http://www.universalbyline.com

Compuserve's Fleet Street Forum
http://www.honk.co.uk/fleetstreet

Creative Freelancers Online
http://www.freelancers.com

The Economist – politics and business commentary
http://www.economist.com

Editor & Publisher magazine online
http://www.mediainfo.com/ephome/index/unihtm

The Electronic Telegraph – news, sports, finance, entertainment
http://www.telegraph.co.uk

The Electronic Newsstand – Includes news and sport; FT stock exchange movements
http://www.enews.com

Eurojournalism
http://www.demon.co.uk/eurojournalism

European Press Network – syndication service (trial)
http://www.epnworld.com

Finding experts – ongoing research and ideas, PR bulletins and much else
http://www.aukml.org.uk

Free Pint – free bi-monthly email newsletter with tips and articles on finding reliable sites and searching more effectively. Written by information professionals
http://www.freepint.co.uk

Grammar for Journalists – course at the university of Oregon but worth looking at for the novice
http://jcomm.uoregon.edu/~kelleew/j101

Guardian and Observer – archive of stories going back to 1 September 1998
http://www.guardianunlimited.co.uk/Archive

HM Stationery Office – many government publications online and searchable database
http://www.parliament.the-stationery-office.co.uk

Internet Markets and Resources for Writers
ftp://rtfm.mit.edu/pub/usenet/news.answers/writing/resources

Investigative Reporters and Editors – database of more than 11,000 investigative reporting story abstracts
http://www.ire.org

Journal of Digital Information – electronic journal supported by the British Computer Society and Oxford University Press
http://jodi.ecs.soton.ac.uk

Lexis-Nexis – databases from over 23,000 news, legal, business and government sources. Pricing is tailored for each firm, company or individual
http://www.lexis-nexis.com/lncc

Magazine and Newsletter Editor Resources
http://www.fileshop.com/personal/tgoff/erlist

Media Centre – vacancies for journalists
http://www.mediamasters.ndirect.co.uk/mediacentre/jobs.htm

The Movie Critic
http://www.moviecritic.com

National Institute for Computer-Assisted Reporting
http://www.nicar.org

NewsAhead – for forward planning
http://www.newsahead.com

NewsIndex – keeps you posted on news articles about subjects you select
http://www.newsindex.com

Newslinks For Journalists – includes links to several hundred newspapers, magazines and broadcasting venues (mostly in the US)
http://www.newslink.org

Newspaper cuttings – free as opposed to the subscription-based Lexis-Nexis
http://metalab.unc.edu/collection

Online Journalism Review
http://ojr.usc.edu/sections/index.shtml

Online Newspapers – print media world-wide
http://ipl.lub.lu.se/cgi-bin/reading/news.out.pl

Out There News – online news agency – run by two ex-Reuters journalists
http://www.outtherenews.com

Press Association News Centre (UK) – latest stories from the UK's top news and information websites; useful free daily round-up of news, sport and information by email
http://www.pa.press.net

Reporters' Resources – a good US-based collection
http://reporter.umd.edu/journ.htm

Response Source – where UK journalists can request information in a single step from over 300 organisations
http://sourcewire.com/frames/pr/index.html

Reuters
http://www.reuters.com

RIG: Reporter's Internet Guide – guide-book for reporters using the Internet
http://www.crl.com/~jshenry/rig.html

The Source – one-stop resource for IT journalists looking for industry quotes
http://thesource.dwpub.com

The Source – website for official UK statistics
http://www.statistics.gov.uk

The Times – full *Times* and *Sunday Times* newspapers
http://www.the-times.co.uk
http://www.sunday-times.co.uk

UK Knowhere Guide – for finding film locations
http://www.knowhere.co.uk

UK newspapers – links to all the national UK press online and several hundred regional online newspapers in England, Scotland, Wales and Ireland
http://www.zen.co.uk/home/page/wrx/alltnews.htm

Willings Press Guide
http://www.hollis-pr.co.uk

Writers@Work – jump site to electronic bulletin boards where publishers, editors and media moguls post job announcements of interest to freelancers
http://www.geteducated.com/wgir_ch3.htm

Literature festivals
Brighton Festival
http://www.brighton-festival.org.uk

Cheltenham Festival of Literature
http://www.cheltenhamfestivals.co.uk

City of London Festival
http://www.city-of-london-festival.org.uk

Edinburgh International Book Festival
http://www.edinburghfestivals.co.uk

Exeter Festival
http://www.exeter.gov.uk

Federation of Worker Writers and Community Publishers Festival of Writing
http://www.fwwcp.mcmail.com

Guildford Book Festival
http://www.surreyweb.org.uk

Harrogate International Festival
http://www.harrogate-festival.org.uk

Ilkley Literature Festival
http://www.ilkley.org/arts/index.htm

Lancaster LitFest
http://www.folly.co.uk/litfest

Norfolk and Norwich Festival
http://www.eab.org.uk/festivals

Ways With Words Literature Festival
http://www.users.globalnet.co.uk/~wwwords

Writearound: Middlesbrough's Annual Festival for Writers and Readers
http://www.clevelandarts.org

Literature resources
Arts Council of England
http://www.artscouncil.org.uk

British Literature resource
http://www.britishliterature.com

Literature online – Chadwyck-Healey
http://lion.chadwyck.co.uk

Literary Arts webring – the art, craft and business of fiction, poetry, essays and creative nonfiction
http://www.lit-arts.com/WebRing

The Literary Menagerie – US author-based sites
http://home.olemiss.edu/~egcash

Mystery
See CRIME WRITING & MYSTERY

Poetry
The Academy of American Poets
http://www.poet.org

Electronic Poetry Center – claims to be the largest poetry web centre in the world, with nearly 20 gigabytes of information in more than 7200 files
http://wings.buffalo.edu/epc

Living Poets
http://dougal.derby.ac.uk/lpoets

Peter Finch Archive – experience the *R S Thomas Information*
http://dialspace.dial.pipex.com/peter.finch

Peter's Poetry Generator – and links to lots of other poetry places
http://www.hphoward.demon.co.uk/poemgen/framset1.htm

Poetry Book Society
http://www.poetrybooks.co.uk

Poetry Express
http://www.ns.net/~Lomar/page2.htm

Poetry Ireland
http://www.poetryireland.ie

The Poetry Library
http://www.poetrylibrary.org.uk

The Poetry Society
http://www.poetrysoc.com

The Poetry Society of America
http://www.poetrysociety.org

Poets & Writers – varied resource for writers of all kinds, sited in the US
http://www.pw.org

Ring of Words – webring with 1000 other linked sites (some personal, some quirky); also has a chat room
http://www.poetrytodayonline.com/words

Rhyming dictionary
http://www.link.cs.cmu.edu/dougb/rhyme-doc.html

Still: the Haiku Resource
http://www.into.demon.co.uk

Word Circuits – interesting poetry and fiction site with lots of other links
http://www.wordcircuits.com

Poetry workshops
John Kinsella's poetryetc@listbot.com
Peter Howard's poetry @lists.cyberware co.uk
http://www.writerswrite.com/poetry/boards. htm

Prizes
$100,000 annual prize for the best book published originally in electronic form; six smaller prizes. 2000 first year – search the Microsoft site for details
http://www.microsoft.com

The Arts Council of Wales Awards to Writers
http://www.ccc-acw.org.uk

Booker Prize – winners and shortlisted
http://www.utc.edu/~engldept/booker/booker. htm

The Bridport Prizes
http://www.wdi.co.uk/arts

CWA Awards
http://www.twbooks.co.uk/cwa/cwa.html

The Dundee Book Prize
shttp://www.dundee.ac.uk/pressreleases/ dunpri.htm
http://dundeecity.gov.uk/dcchtml/cofd/ bookprize.html

The Hans Christian Andersen Medals
http://www.ibby.org

International IMPAC Dublin Literary Award
http://www.iol.ie/~dubcilib

The Library Association Carnegie and Kate Greenaway Awards
http://www.la-hq.org.uk

National Poetry Competition
http://www.poetrysoc.com

Orange Prize for Fiction
http://www.orange.co.uk/prize/index.html

Pen American Center – awards, grants, literary prizes, freedom to write
http://www.pen.org

Pulitzer Prizes
http://www.pulitzer.org

The Rhône-Poulenc Prizes for Science Books
http://www.royalsoc.ac.uk

The Scottish Book of the Year and Scottish First Book
http://www.saltire-society.demon.co.uk

Whitbread Book Awards
http://www.whitbread.co.uk

Romance
All About Romance – romance readers' home for romance novels, romance reviews, romance news, romance authors
http://www.likesbooks.com/home.html

Orpheus Romance – stories for women; writers paid advances and a 30% royalty
http://www.orpheusromance.com

Romance Central
http://romance-central.com/index1.htm

The Romance Club
http://www.theromanceclub.com

Romance Newsgroups and Listservs
http://www.geocities.com/Athens/8774/listsv. htm

Romance Writers of America
http://www.rwanational.com

Romantic Ghosts and Gothics
http://www.autopen.com/ghost.gothic.shtml

Ultimate Romance Novel Website
http://www.icgnet.com/romancebooks

Mary Wolf's guide to electronic publishers; personal links for submission for romance writers
http://www.coredcs.com/~mermaid/epub.html

Science fiction, fantasy and horror

Ansible – archive of links, including to well-known authors writing in the genre
http://www.dcs.gla.ac.uk/SF-Archives/Ansible/ansilink.html

British Fantasy Society
http://www.geocities.com/SoHo/6859

British Science Fiction Association
http://www.members.aol.com/tamaranth

Event Horizon
http://www.e-horizon.com/eventhorizon

The Exploratorium
http://www.exploratorium.org

Fantasy & Horror readers
http://www.phantastes.com

Infinity Plus
http://www.users.zetnet.co.uk/iplus

Links to authors' sites
http://www.iplus.zetnet.co.uk/misc/authsite.htm

Locus Online
http://www.locusmag.com

Rutgers SF-Lovers archive
http://sflovers.rutgers.edu

Science Fiction and Fantasy sites – a collection
http://www.okima.com/book/links.html
Science Fiction resources
http://www.forwriters.com

Science Fiction Writers Association
http://www.sfwa.org

Science Fiction Writers of Earth (SFWoE)
http://www.flash.net/~sfwoe

Science Fiction Zone
http://www.lineone.net

Tangent
http://www.sfsite.com/tangent

Tor SF and Fantasy page – other links
http://www.tor.com/tor.html

Specialist subjects

Food, sport, gender and other specialist writers are not necessarily represented individually. Try under search engines or:

Subject-based gateways – clearing houses to quality assessed Internet resources
http://www.lub.lu.se/desire/sbigs.html

STM (Scientific, Technical and Medical) writers

There are countless scientific, technical and medical journals and Internet resources in these fields. These are just starting points.

American Medical Writers Association
http://www.amwa.org

Association for Information Management
http://www.aslib.co.uk

Association of British Science Writers (ABSW)
http://www.esf.org/eusja/absw.htm

Association of Health Care Journalists (US)
http://metalab.unc.edu/namc

BioTech's Life Science Dictionary – 6000 + terms used in biochemistry, biotechnology, botany, cell biology and genetics
http://biotech.icmb.utexas.edu

Board of Editors in the Life Sciences
http://www.bels.org

British Medical Association – part of the site is for journalists
http://www.bma.org.uk

Current Contents – from current awareness database at the Institute for Scientific Information providing information in the fields of science, social science, technology, and arts and humanities
http://www.isinet.com/prodserv/cc/cchp.html

Drugs – InteliHealth – Home to Johns Hopkins Health Information Drug Resource Center
http://www.intelihealth.com/IH

Eurekalert – offers free (passworded) online access to the latest research findings

in science, medicine technology and health
http://www.eurekalert.org

European Association of Science Editors
http://www.ease.org.uk

European Union of Science Writers
http://www.esf.org/eusja/websites.htm

GeoGuide – geography and earth sciences information gateway
http://www.sub.uni-goettingen.de/ssgfi/geo/index.html

The Institute of Information Scientists – professional association for people involved in creating, retrieving, organising or disseminating information
http://www.iis.org.uk

List of Journals Indexed in Index Medicus
http://www.nlm.nih.gov/tsd/serials/lji.html

Medline – there are several free gateways to Medline; not all the same in functionality
http://www4.ncbi.nlm.nih.gov/PubMed

MedWeb
http://www.emory.edu

Multilingual Glossary of medical terms
http://allserv.rug.ac.be/~rvdstich/eugloss/welcome.html

Nature
http://www.nature.com

New Scientist
http://www.newscientist.com/home.html

Online Medical Dictionary – excellent searchable, browsable dictionary of more than 46,000 entries, part of CancerNet
http://www.graylab.ac.uk/omd

Science Direct – research texts in 14 fields of science; mostly Elsevier and other STM publishers
http://www.sciencedirect.com

Science & Technology links – access to goverment selected sites
http://www.earl.org.uk/earlweb/science.html

SOSIG – Social Science Information Gateway
http://www.sosig.ac.uk

Technical writing
See also WEB WRITING (7)

Information Design – electronic publications and computer-based learning programs
http://www.mantex.co.uk

One-stop resource for IT journalists looking for industry quotes
http://thesource.dwpub.com

Online Dictionary of Computing – quantities of definitions of terms; some really strange ones
http://foldoc.doc.ic.ac.uk/foldoc/index.html

Society for Technical Communication (US) – searchable database of publications
http://www.stc-va.org/default.htm

Society of Technical and Scientific Communicators (UK) – conferences, courses, articles, etc.
http://www.istc.org.uk

Technical Writing – a mine of information
http://techwriting.miningco.com

Screen, TV and playwriting
See also WRITING TOOLS for software templates

BBC
http://www.bbc.co.uk
BBC Entertainment
http://www.comedyzone.beeb.com /writestuff

Britcomedy Digest – newsletter archive, suspended in 1999 but may revive
http://www.prairienet.org/britcom/BD/index.html

The British Comedy Library
http://www.michael.phatcatz.net/awtv/Comedy/index.html

British Theatre – everything on the theatre you could possibly want
http://britishtheatre.miningco.com

Community Writers Association – US model which could give the Brits a few ideas
http://www.communitywriters.org/index2.html

Drama on the Web
http://www.thestage.co.uk

E-Script – internet scriptwriting workshop
http://www.singlelane.com/escript

Essays on the Craft of Dramatic Writing
http://www.teleport.com/~bjscript/index.htm

Euroscript – media project of the EU to advance European scriptwriting in the form of distance training that develops scripts; reads, selects and promotes scripts and writers; and supports writers' groups
http://www.euroscript.co.uk

Independent Radio Drama Productions
http://www.irdp.co.uk/index.htm

Internet Movie Database – an Internet Halliwell
http://www.imdb.com

Internet Screenwriter's Network – Hollywood services and products. Access to writing software
http://www.screenwriters.com/screennet.html

National Association of Television Program Executives (NATPE) – non-profit TV programming and software association dedicated to the continued growth and success of the global TV marketplace
http://www.natpe.org

The Nine-Act Structure – a story-structure class for writers and film buffs
http://www.dsiegel.com/film/nine_act.html

Pen & Sword Hypersite
http://www.rahul.net/jag

Playwrights on the Web – a database of plays and playwrights (mostly for directors)
http://www.stageplays.com/writers.htm

The Playwrights Project
http://www.vnet.net/users/phisto

The Professional Screenwriter Links Page
http://members.aol.com/linkwrite/profwrt.html

Screenwriters Online – Screenwriters' network – US-based for professionals and amateurs

http://www.screenwriter.com/insider/news.html

Screenwriters' and Playwrights' Page
http://www.teleport.com/~cdeemer/scrwriter.html

Screenwriters' Workshop, London – devoted to the promotion of new screenwriters
http://www.lsw.org.uk

Script Shop
http://www.scriptshop.com

Shooting People – UK resource for filmmakers, scriptwriters, producers, arts funding bodies, film crew, financiers, actors, cinematographers and agents. Has a daily small ads mailing list
http://www.shootingpeople.org

Sitcom Writing Discussion List – discussion list for working and aspiring sitcom writers
http://www.tvtix.com/sitcom

Story Web – a structure resource for film and multimedia
http://www.dsiegel.com/storyweb.html

Theatre Web – UK resources
http://www.uktw.co.uk

TV Writers Homepage
http://www.tvwriter.com

UK Scriptwriters Network
http://www.darkin.demon.co.uk

Virtual Scriptwriters Workshop – with details of up and coming competitions
http://www.moviebytes.com/mb_home.cfm

Writers Website – entertainment and outlets
http://www.writerswebsite.com

Translation

Free Translation – not bad; paste in a bit of text and try it (two-way French, German, Italian, German, Spanish and Portuguese)
http://www.freetranslation.com

Institute of Translators and Interpreters
http://www.iti.org.uk

International Collegiate of Literary Translators
http://www.euk-straelen.de

Language Today – online magazine for the language industries
http://www.logos.it/language_today

Linguists Online – database of worldwide translators
http://www.users.zetnet.co.uk/bywater/www.linguists.com/home.sht

Systran Translation software – as used on the AltaVista search engine; download it (for a modest fee) or translate web pages on the fly
http://www.systransoft.com/personal.html

Translation Programs – commercial product range
http://www.globalink.com

The Translators Home Companion – information for professional translators and those seeking translation services
http://www.lai.com/lai/companion.html

Translator's Home Page – for professional translators and those who need translations
http://www.rahul.net/lai/companion.html

UK job search site – job advertisements in a number of different categories
http://www.workweb.co.uk

World Language Pages – materials for language learning
http://www.livjm.ac.uk/language

Dictionaries
EURODICAUTOM online dictionary – one of the most comprehensive online dictionaries; lots of subjects to choose from and pleasant to use
http://www2.echo.lu/edic

Multilingual PC Directory – source-guide to foreign language software
http://www.knowledge.co.uk

Online Dictionaries – 500 dictionaries in 140 different languages
http://www.bucknell.edu/~rbeard/diction.html

The Ultimate Word Hoard – several hundred dictionaries
http://www.onelook.com

A Web of On-line Dictionaries – linked to 600 dictionaries in 150 different languages
http://www.facstaff.bucknell.edu/rbeard/diction.html

Travel writing
Local Times Around the World
http://www.hilink.com.au/times

Map collections
http://www.lib.utexas.edu/Libs/PCL/Map_collection/Map_collection.html

On The Road – tips about mobile computing and other links
http://www.slip.net/%7Eokumura/ontheroad.html

Travel Writer's Resources
http://www.city.net

The Virtual Tourist – places all over the world plus email address search facility
http://www.vtourist.com

World Wide Brochures – 15,000 maps and brochures updated daily
http://www.wwb.com

Writing tools
Screenwriting
Dramatica – screenplay software; not free – compare it with ScreenForge below
http://www.dramatica.com

FinalDraft – apparently the bees knees of scripting software – expensive (about £150), high functionality and cross-platform compatibility
http://www.finaldraft.com

Hollywood Screenwriter – apparently very like FinalDraft but a third of the price
http://www.writerspage.com/hsbase.htm

ScreenForge – almost free Hollywood scriptwriting format bolt-on for Word
http://www.execpc.com/~jesser

Scrnplay.dot – free template for Word 6/7 for screenplay writers; both this and

ScreenForge are worth looking at
http://www.erols.com/lehket/Dale/scrnplay.
html

Writers' Guild of America guide to writing software – very sensible advice
http://www.wga.org./tools/ScriptSoftware

Storyware

Alice – software program for storyboard modelling; quite technical but interesting
http://www.cs.virginia.edu/~alice

Brutus Story Generator
http://www.rpi.edu/dept/ppcs/BRUTUS/
brutus.html#Sample

Creativity Unleashed – software to stimulate creative thinking, orginally intended for business
http://www.cul.co.uk

Creativity Web – resources for creativity and innovation; emphasis on lateral thinking
http://www.ozemail.com.au/~caveman/
Creative

Storycraft – writing software for stories
http://www.writerspage.com

Storycraft Writer's Software – fiction-writing program that claims to turn ideas into complete novels/screenplays/plays/short stories
http://www.storycraft-soft.com

Web Store for Writers and Creative Pros – Plots Unlimited, Writer's Software Companion and other software aids
http://www.masterfreelancer.com

Writers' Software – some dedicated items such as plot assistants
http://www.leonardo.net/starcomp/plots.html

Writers' Software Companion –
http://www.novalearn.com/sites/ink.htm

Writer's Toolbox – software resources for writers with slightly annoying advertising
http://www.geocities.com/Athens/6346

Miscellany

Bibliographic software – advanced tools such as Reference Manager, ProCite and EndNote at a price (free trials)
http://www.isinet.com/products/refman.html

Endnote – bibliographical software
http://www.niles.com

Mind Mapping – software to help individuals organise, generate and learn ideas and information; free trial available
http://www.mindman.co.uk

PostIt Notes – just like the paper ones and good for quick notes; 30-day downloadable free trial
http://www.3m.com

Tricks and Trinkets – to make word-processing easier, e.g. autotext for often-used phrases
http://www.tricksandtrinkets.com/pk

WordTips – how to get the best out of Microsoft Word; lots of useful tips, many a real boon for writers
http://www.VitalNews.com/wordtips

Writers Tools – yet more links
http://writetools.com

Speech and handwriting

Dyslectech – resource of technology-based tools to help dyslexic people write; good on dictation systems and speech feedback (of use to those with RSI too)
http://www.dyslexic.com

Dragon Dictate – dictation software; I've used this and it is very good, but I don't like talking to a computer
http://www.dragonsys.ca

Handwriting Repair – improve your writing
http://www.global2000.net/handwritingrepair

My Speech – buttons to add to websites so visitors can ask questions by voice
http://www.myspeech.com/about.htm

Speech Recognition
http://www.speechrecognition.com

Telephony – voice telephone access to your site
http://www.speechtml.com

Voice Recognition links
http://www.tiac.net/users/rwilcox/speech.html

7. Internet publishing practicalities

Bookselling online

Book searching

Acses – book price search engine which compares offers from 23 Internet bookstores. Acses finds the Internetwide best offer for mainstream books in a few seconds
http://www.acses.com

Amazon Bookshop UK – gave the fastest service in my (somewhat random) testing
http://www.amazon.co.uk

Amazon Bookshop US
http://www.amazon.com

Author's Showcase – online bookstore of published and self-published authors; book jackets, author biographies and sampler text
http://www.authorshowcase.com

BOL – Bertelsmann OnLine
http://www.bol.com

Book Arts Links – links to a large selection of book arts related sites on the web
http://www.dreamscape.com/pdverhey

The Bookpl@ce – searchable by chapter heading too; links to choice of suppliers
http://www.thebookplace.co.uk

Books Wire
http://www.booksinprint.com

Bookshop for the Book Business – specialist publications, reports and market intelligence to the book publishing, distribution and retail industry
http://www.theBookseller.com/shop

Bookwire – reviews, publishing news, bestseller lists, an author tour calendar and other links
http://www.bookwire.com

Broadcast.com – audio-books to listen to online or buy the cassettes; good range of titles; other broadcasting services too
http://www.broadcast.com

Email directory of people in publishing
http://www.anagram.net/bic

Fire and Water – community for book people, mostly HarperCollins
http://www.fireandwater.com

Heffers – Cambridge, UK
http://www.heffers.co.uk

Internet Bookshop
http://www.bookshop.co.uk

National History Bookservice – vast catalogue specialising in natural history and ecology
http://www.nhbs.co.uk

Penguin
http://www.penguin.co.uk

Waterstone's Bookshop
http://www.waterstones.co.uk

WH Smith – mixed portal for arts and education http://www.whsmith.co.uk

Antiquarian and bookbinding

Adrian Harrington – antiquarian bookseller
http://dialspace.dial.pipex.com/town/drive/gbg94

Bibliofind – claims to be able to find any book available for sale
http://www.bibliofind.com

Imperial Fine Books Inc – New York
http://www.dir-dd.com/imperial-fine-books.html

Jonathan A. Hill, Bookseller Inc. – New York
http://www.abaa-booknet.com/usa/j.hill

The Society of Bookbinders – dedicated to traditional bookbinding, preserving and conserving the printed and written word
http://www.socbkbind.com

Ursus Books – New York
http://www.ursusbooks.com

Wilsey Rare Books – New York
http://www.clark.net/pub/wilsey

Legal deposit

British Library – follow the Collections and the Digital Library tabs
http://www.bl.uk

Working Party on Legal Deposit
http://www.culture.gov.uk/LDWGRPT.HTM

E-commerce

BarclaySquare – UK's first online shopping mall; has micropayment scheme
http://www.barclaysquare.co.uk

Building confidence in e-commerce
http://www.dti.gov.uk/cii/elec/ecbill.html

Electronic Commerce Association UK
http://www.eca.org.uk

Electronic Communications Bill – Government drafts
http://www.dti.gov.uk/cii/elec/ecbill.html

Government White Paper on the business potential of the Internet
http://www.uu.net/info/english/en_index.htm

Interactive Web-based government services
http://www.open.gov.uk

MyPublish – e-commerce partner for the aspiring entrepreneur – where publishing creativity and making a profit live in harmony on the web; their blurb
http://www.mypublish.com/mypublish

National Institute of Standards and Technology
http://www.nist.gov

NUA: Internet Strategy & Development – excellent site giving Internet statistics and opinion
http://www.nua.ie

PublishOne – to sell or control distribution of financial and investment information, research reports, newsletters, or technical and academic journals
http://www.publishone.com

UK Communities Online – not-for-profit organisation which exists to harness the potential of information and communications technology for the benefit of all
http://www.communities.org.uk

Universal Currency Converter – real time conversions to aid Internet shopping
http://www.xe.net/currency

YBP Publishing Services – developing electronic publishing and copyright management solutions for publishers and users
http://www.ybp.com/yps

Security

Cash and credit cards

MilliCent – microcommerce system for trading in small denominations; uses electronic coupons called scrip which represents money
http://www.millicent.digital.com

NetBanx – a UK Internet equivalent of the card swipe machines used by retailers when processing payment by credit or debit cards
http://www.netbanx.com

NextPage – secure pathways into the future of electronic publishing; mainly business focus
http://www.nextpage.com

Qpass – allows you to charge for online content and takes a percentage of your sales in something it calls 'Point, click, purchase' technology
http://www.qpass.com

Secure Socket Layer technology information
http://www.visa.com
http://www.mastercard.com
http://www.americanexpress.com

Secure Trading – UK service for processing credit card payments on websites
http://www.securetrading.com

WorldPay – UK-based, multicurrency site in association with NatWest; one off set up fee and then a percentage of each transaction on credit card transactions
http://www.worldpay.com

Filtering software

I-Gear – content management software suite; not quite in the individual writer's league, but a serious filtering system for a school, college or large company
http://www.urlabs.com/public

NetNanny – filtering software for home and schools
http://www.netnanny.com

SafeSurf
http://www.safesurf.com

Privacy

Electronic Privacy Information Center
http://www.epic.org

Guidelines on Privacy and Security
http://www.oecd.org/dsti/sti/it/secur/prod

Guidelines on Protection of Personal Data
http://www.ecom.or.jp/eng/output/wg12/wg12guidline.htm

Marketing

Author Interviews.Com – designed exclusively to help authors get interviews to promote their books on US radio and TV; a splendid idea which someone should emulate for the UK
http://www.authorinterviews.com

BookMarket – marketing articles and ideas
http://www.bookmarket.com

Books A to Z – Internet marketing and publication resources
http://www.booksatoz.com

Books in Print
http://www.bowker.com/bip

Cassell Network of Writers – linking professional writers with those who hire writers and editorial help; part of the site is free; part subscribers only
http://writers-editors.com

Digital Aesthetics – an academic writer's style of try-before-you buy self-promotion; see if it gives you ideas
http://www.ucl.ac.uk/slade/digita

Idea Marketers – free place to post your articles and get exposure but there's no mention of fees
http://www.ideamarketers.com

ISSN Online – authoritative source of ISSN and serials information; some free, some paid, access
http://www.issn.org

Mantex – electronic publishing consultancy, with free newsletters and useful book reviews
http://www.mantex.co.uk

Literary Market Place Online – portal for information about the book publishing industry
http://www.literarymarketplace.com

Marketing Online – collection of onsite articles offering quite useful advice
http://bookzonepro.com

Sell More Books – one of those '27 ways to market your book' pages; could possibly trigger an unthought-of seam
http://www.idealady.com/sellmore.htm

Sensible Solutions to getting happily published – sane advice with US-based links
http://www.happilypublished.com

Publishing

See Publishers Association for access to British publishers online.

Association of Little Presses (ALP) – for small and self-publishers
http://www.melloworld.com/alp

Authorlink – site for editors, agents, writers; includes section on self-published books for sale; based in Dallas
http://www.authorlink.com

BIC (Book Industry Communications)
http://www.bic.org.uk

Book Trust
http://dspace.dial.pipex.com/booktrust

Booksellers Association of Great Britain & Ireland
http://www.booksellers.org.uk

BookWeb – service provided by Sweetens Computer Services to allow smaller publishers to have a web presence
http://www.bookweb.co.uk

BookWire
http://www.bookwire.com

iCopyright.com – aiming to clear copyright permissions and reprints from any

registered publisher
http://www1.icopyright.com/index.html

Directory & Database Publishers Association
http://www.directory-publisher.co.uk

Multiquotes – free service submitting printing requirements to UK printing companies for anything from printed brochures and leaflets to printed umbrellas. The companies email back a quote
http://www.multiquotes.co.uk

Periodical Publishers Association
http://www.asa.org.uk/bcasp/r_ppa.htm

Pira International – very useful information on the printing industries
http://www.pira.co.uk

Pub Space – about the transformation of books through the use of electronic media; who's doing what, what possibilities are available and where you should direct your attention
http://www.pubspace.com

Publishers Association – links to all UK publishers who are members of the PA
http://www.publishers.org.uk/Directory

Publisher's Catalogues HomePages
http://www.lights.com/publisher

Publishing News online – news of the UK book trade
http://www.publishingnews.co.uk

Scottish Book Trust
http://www.webpost.net/bts

Scottish Publishers Association
http://www.scottishbooks.org

Self-Publishers Discussion List – newsletter-style list where self-publishing authors discuss marketing, profit and production strategies
http://www.writersmarkets.com/index-publish.htm

Society of Young Publishers
http://www.thesyp.demon.co.uk

Spoken Word Publishing Association
http://www.swpa.org.uk

Whitakers – information service provider for the UK book industry
http://www.whitaker.co.uk/

Writer's Loft – featuring the business side of writing, including articles and ePublishing industry news
http://www.ebookconnections.com/writersloft/wl_home.htm

Writers' Pad – a site where you can submit fiction and get paid for it
http://tale.com/writech.phtml

Web writing
See also WEB ACCESS TOOLS (1) and CHAT (4)

Alert Box – web usability and readability theory
http://www.useit.com/alertbox

Ameritech Web Page User Interface and Design Guidelines
http://www.ameritech.com/corporate/testtown/library/standard/web_guidelines/reference.html

Coffee Cup – web creation tools
http://www.coffeecup.com

Cyberguide for Search Engine Promotion
http://www.rankthis.com

Network Solutions – to check the availability of domain names
http://www.netsol.com
or
http://www.allwhois.com

Nominet – to register a British domain name
http://www.nominet.org.uk

Poor Richard's Web links – another 800 or so excellent links all about writing and maintaining web pages
http://www.poorrichard.com/links/index.html

Reading and skimming from computer screens
http://psych.utoronto.ca/~muter/pmuter2.htm

Site Aid – freeware HTML editor; looks quite like Microsoft's FrontPage
http://www.siteaid.com

Tips for Writers and Designers – from David Siegel's book
http://www.dsiegel.com/tips

UK2.Net - inexpensive domain registration and web forwarding
http://uk2.net

Virtual Promote for website promotion tips and ideas
http://www.virtualpromote.com

Web Reference – all the latest authoring tools
http://webreference.com

Web Site Promotion
http://www.register-it.com

Web Style Guide: Basic Design Principles for Creating Web Sites (Yale University Press in March 1999 online version)
http://info.med.yale.edu/caim/manual
/contents.html

Weekend Webmaster tools
http://www.zdnet.com/swlib/toolkits/
webmast/tlk0698.html

Wired News
http://www.wired.com

Write-Link
http://www.linkcheck.co.uk/writelink

Writing for the Web by Jacob Nielsen
http://www.sun.com/980713/webwriting

Yale Style Manual – excellent guide to various aspects of web writing
http://info.med.yale.edu/caim/manual

HTML *resources*
The HTML Writers Guild – free membership and access to resources
http://www.hwg.org

HTML 4.0 Specification – official specification for HTML from the World Wide Web Consortium
http://www.w3.org/TR/REC-html40

Cascading Style Sheets Specification (CSS1) – official guidelines with links to tutorials
http://www.w3.org/Style/CSS

Index DOT Html – comprehensive listing of HTML tags and their compatibility with the various browsers
http://www.blooberry.com/html

Web Review's Style Sheets Reference Guide – what styles are and in which browsers they work
http://webreview.com/guides/style/style.html

Scripts
The CGI Resource Index – scripts that you can buy (some free) e.g. form-handling, guest books and counters
http://www.cgi-resources.com

JavaScript Cut & Paste
http://www.infohiway.com/javascript/indexf.htm

Matt's Script Archive
http://www.worldwidemart.com/scripts

Tagging
Dublin Core Metadata Initiative
http://purl.oclc.org/dc

The World Wide Web Consortium: Metadata and Resource Description
http://www.w3.org/Metadata

8. Issues in an online environment

Copyright and protection
Copyright Societies
http://www.cisac.org

Digital Watermarking Site
http://www.bluespike.com

Directive on Copyright and Related Rights in the Information Society – latest news
http://www.patent.gov.uk/dpolicy/infosoc1.html

Essays in post-modernism and copyright
http://www.arts.ucsb.edu/~tvc/v10/index.html

Fair Dealing in an electronic environment – Joint Information Systems Committee and Publishers Association 1998
http://www.ukoln.ac.uk/services/elib/papers/
pa/fair/intro.html

Future of Intellectual Property in an Online World (Bird & Bird library paper)
http://www.twobirds.com/library/internet/online.htm

Intellectual Property Rights issues –comprehensive information on the benefits and practical aspects of IPR protection in Europe
http://www.cordis.lu/ipr-helpdesk/enhome.htm

Lawtel – provider of online legal information; free trial available
http://www.lawtel.co.uk

Model standard licences for use by publishers, librarians and subscription agents for electronic resources
http://www.licensingmodels.com

The Patent Office (UK) – a wide range of information and a well-designed site
http://www.patent.gov.uk

SICI – Serial Item and Contribution Identifier Standard; a numbering system to watch
http://sunsite.berkeley.edu/SICI

US Association of Research Libraries
http://arl.cni.org/info/frn/copy/copytoc.html

US Copyright Office – find the latest on the Digital Millennium Copyright Act
http://lcweb.loc.gov/copyright

Watch – Writers, Artists and Their Copyright Holders searchable database is a joint project of the Universities of Reading and Texas; archiving and library focus
http://www.lib.utexas.edu/Libs/HRC/WATCH

WIPO – World Intellectual Property Organization
http://www.wipo.org

Privacy
See E-COMMERCE (7)

Societies and writers' organisations in the UK

Societies and unions
ALCS – The Authors' Licensing and Collecting Society (UK) – has a mandate to collect money for photocopying and electronic rights on behalf of writers
http://www.alcs.co.uk

ALPSP – Association of Learned and Professional Society Publishers
http://www.alpsp.org.uk

Alliance of Literary Societies
http://www.sndc.demon.co.uk/als.htm

British Educational Communications and Technology agency (BECTa)
http://www.becta.org.uk

Broadcasting Entertainment Cinematograph and Theatre Union (BECTU) – union for media people
http://www.gn.apc.org/media/bectu.html

The Chartered Institute of Journalists – society representing employed and freelance journalists in the UK
http://www.users.dircon.co.uk/~cioj

CLA The Copyright Licensing Society – photocopying and electronic licensing agency
http://clans.cla.co.uk/www/index.html

Internet Writers Guild – non-commercial association of writers and artists who use the Internet to publish their work; starting point for the Internet public looking for free art (both visual and literary) on the web
http://members.tripod.com/~IWG

The National Union of Journalists – society representing employed and freelance journalists in the UK
http://www.gn.apc.org/media/nuj.html

The Society of Authors – society representing 7000 authors
http://www.writers.org.uk/society

SPELL (Society for the Preservation of English Language and Literature)
http://www.mindspring.com/~spellorg

Translation & Interpreting, The Institute of (ITI)
http://www.iti.org.uk

The Writers' Guild of Great Britain
http://www.writers.org.uk/guild

General

Arts Council of England
http://www.artscouncil.org.uk

The British Council
http://www.britcoun.org

Contemporary Arts, Institute of
http://www.illumin.co.uk/ica
History of Authorship, Reading & Publishing, Society for the
http://www.indiana.edu/~sharp

The Library Association
http://www.la-hq.org.uk

Literary Societies, Alliance of
http://www.sndc.demon.co.uk

National Campaign for the Arts (NCA)
http://www.artscampaign.org

Pen UK
http://www.pen.org.uk

Periodical Publishers Association
http://www.ppa.co.uk

The Press Complaints Commission
http://www.pcc.org.uk

Public Lending Right
http://www.earl.org.uk/partners/plr/index.html

The Reading Experience Database 1450–1914 (RED)
http://www2.open.ac.uk/arts/RED

Regional Arts Boards (RABs)
http://www.arts.org.uk

Scottish Newspaper Publishers Association
http://www.snpa.org.uk

Scottish Publishers Association
http://www.scottishbooks.org

Special interest

The Jane Austen Society
http://www.sndc.demon.co.uk/jas.htm

Thomas Lovell Beddoes Society
http://www.nortexinfo.net/mcdaniel

The Brontë Society
http://www.bronte.org.uk

The Eckhart Society
http://www.op.org/eckhart

The Eighteen Nineties Society
http://www.1890s.org

English Association
http://www.le.ac.uk/engassoc
Fantasy Society, The British
http://www.geocities.com/soho/6859

Historical Novel Society
http://www.ex.ac.uk/histnov

The Sherlock Holmes Society of London
http://www.sherlock-holmes.org.uk

Journalists, National Council for the Training of
http://www.itecharlow.co.uk/nctj

The Kipling Society
http://www.kipling.org.uk

The John Masefield Society
http://www.ucl.ac.uk/~uczzpwe/jms1.htm

National Association of Writers in Education (NAWE)
http://www.nawe.co.uk

New Science Fiction Alliance (NSFA)
http://www.bbr-online.com/catalogue

Outdoor Writers' Guild
http://www.owg.org.uk

The Powys Society
http://www.iaehv.nl/users/tklijn/pws/powys.htm

The Dorothy L. Sayers Society
http://www.sayers.org.uk

Angela Thirkell Society
http://www.angelathirkell.org

The Tolkien Society
http://www.tolkiensociety.org

Mary Webb Society
http://www.wlv.qc.uk/~me1927/m.webb.html

Women in Publishing
http://www.cyberiacafe.net/wip

Worker Writers and Community Publishers, The Federation of
http://www.fwwcp.mcmail.com

Health
Patient UK – authenticated health portal for search queries of all kinds
http://www.patient.co.uk

RSI/UK – good starting point
http://www.demon.co.uk/rsi

see also STM Writers (page 182)

Index